HUMOROUS, SERIOUS, CHALLENGING, FUN!

TEST YOUR BIBLE POWER

challenges your knowledge of the Bible through all kinds of games and puzzles. You'll discover wonderful bits of trivia, while learning about the "Good Book."

TEST YOUR BIBLE POWER

- Numbers, Dates, and Other Important Facts
- Who's Who: The Famous and the Forgotten
- Decisions That Shaped History
- Memorable Comments
- Prophecies and Promises
- Commandments and Curses
- Sins and Other Faults
- Places That Time Passed By
- Miracles and the Supernatural
- Complete Your Favorite Bible Passage

TEST YOUR BIBLE POWER

TEST YOUR
BIBLE POWER

Hastings House
A Division of United Publishers Group
Norwalk, CT

Hastings House
A Division of United Publishers Group
50 Washington Street
Norwalk, CT 06854

ISBN: 0-8038-9397-3

Library of Congress Catalog Card Number 97-071275

Distributed to the trade by Publishers Group West, Emeryville, CA

Test Your Bible Power, Multiple choice questions 1-5,
13-32, 37-60, 69-88, 93-121, 126-149, 154-172, 177-200,
209-220, 226-228, 233-236, 241-248, 257-268, 273-284

All quotations are from the King James Version of the Bible

Printed in the United States of America

10 9 8 7 6 5 4 3 2 1

CONTENTS

TEST YOUR BIBLE POWER

The idea for *Test Your Bible Power* came from Jerome Agel, who, with Eugene Boe, launched the book with a sampling of multiple choice questions.

Of course, you can't very well test yourself without a scoring system. While you can grade yourself on the puzzles and games, we suggest the following for the multiple choice questions. There are 284 total multiple choice questions.

below 175 . . . Average. Biblical scholarship is not your forte. You can either do some brushing up on the Word or simply reflect that a high score is not to be equated with godliness.

176–225 . . . Good! You've got a handle on the "good book," though it's premature to let yourself be flattered for your knowledge.

226–275 . . . Excellent! You're a connoisseur of the Word. With a little luck you might be able to market your expertise.

276–284 . . . You had to have been there! If you're not a recognized Biblical scholar, you've missed your calling.

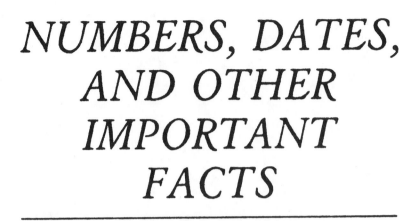

NUMBERS, DATES, AND OTHER IMPORTANT FACTS

Why were his brothers trying to kill him?

(Answers to the puzzles in Chapter 1 can be found on pages 169–171.)

1. If you will read the Bible from cover to cover, how many books will you have read?

   a. 57

   b. 61

   c. 66

   d. 72

2. The Israelites dwelt in Egypt for _____.

   a. 40 years

   b. 120 years

   c. 430 years

   d. a millennium

3. Methuselah has long been renowned as the oldest man who ever lived—969 years. Jared, the second oldest, lived how long?

   a. 740 years

   b. 763 years

   c. 875 years

   d. 962 years

4. How many sons did Adam and Eve have?

   a. one

   b. two

   c. three

   d. many

3

5. With Noah and family safely in the ark, the rains lasted 40 days and 40 nights. How long was it until the waters receded?

   a. one week

   b. 40 days

   c. 150 days

   d. one year

6. With the Midianites poised for an invasion of Israel, Gideon rounded up an army of 32,000 men. However, God's idea of a counteroffensive was to reduce the army to

   a. 70 men

   b. 300 men

   c. 1,000 men

   d. 5,000 men

7. King Hezekiah, gravely ill, was told by the prophet Isaiah that he was about to die. Hezekiah pleaded for an extension to his life. How many years did God then add to his life?

   a. 1

   b. 5

   c. 15

   d. 40

8. How many books of the Bible begin with the words "In the beginning"...?

   a. 1

   b. 2

   c. 3

   d. 6

4

9. The longest chapter in the Bible is _____.

   a. Proverbs 9

   b. Psalms 119

   c. Genesis 24

   d. Psalms 91

10. The shortest chapter in the Bible is _____.

    a. Proverbs 7

    b. Psalms 127

    c. Psalms 17

    d. Psalms 117

11. The longest verse in the Bible is _____.

    a. Revelation 22:18

    b. Ecclesiastes 6:12

    c. Esther 8:9

    d. Psalms 150:6

12. The shortest verse in the Bible is _____.

    a. Jesus wept.

    b. I know not.

    c. Come, Lord.

    d. He said.

13. Before the New Testament was composed, the Old Testament was called _____.

    a. The Gospel of Moses and the Prophets

    b. The Law and the Prophets

    c. The Torah and the Commandments

    d. The History of the Chosen People

14. In Greek, the language of the New Testament, the word "Gospel" means _____.

    a. The Synoptic

    b. The Eyewitness

    c. The Truth

    d. Good News

15. In a parable in Judges, the trees decide to choose a king. The olive, the fig, and the vine refuse the offer to reign. Finally the _____agrees to serve.

    a. mangrove

    b. poplar

    c. cedar of Lebanon

    d. bramble

THE BOOKS OF THE BIBLE

The criss-cross puzzle on the opposite page contains the names of all the books of the Bible. There are no duplicates. The words *First, Second,* and *Third* are not listed. Thus, the word *John* (as shown) appears only once. Note, too, that the Song of Solomon appears as Solomon.

Genesis	Nehemiah	Hosea
Exodus	Esther	Joel
Leviticus	Job	Amos
Numbers	Psalms	Obadiah
Deuteronomy	Proverbs	Jonah
Joshua	Ecclesiastes	Micah
Judges	Solomon	Nahum
Ruth	Isaiah	Habakkuk
Samuel	Jeremiah	Zephaniah
Kings	Lamentations	Haggai
Chronicles	Ezekiel	Zechariah
Ezra	Daniel	Malachi

Matthew
Mark
Luke
John
Acts
Romans
Corinthians

Galatians
Ephesians
Philippians
Colossians
Thessalonians
Timothy
Titus

Philemon
Hebrews
James
Peter
Jude
Revelation

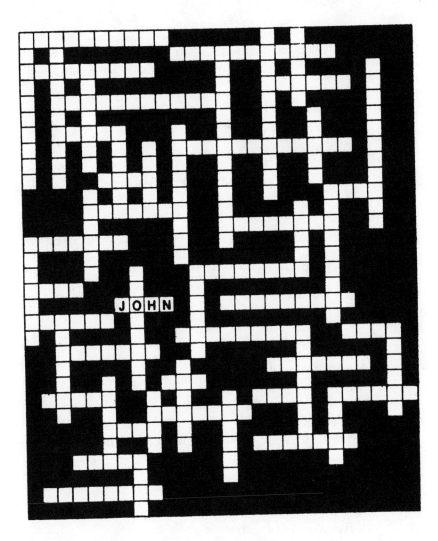

16. The first five books of the Old Testament are collectively known as _____.

    a. the Torah

    b. the Laws of Abraham

    c. the Covenant

    d. the Book of Knowledge

17. Even Pharaoh could not marry off a daughter without a dowry; the dowry of Solomon's bride was _____.

    a. 75,000 slaves

    b. the ruined city of Gezer

    c. 20,000 chariots

    d. cedar wood and gold for the new temple

18. Joseph's jealous brothers, who had sold him into slavery, unexpectedly ran into him again in Egypt. The agent of their reconciliation was _____.

    a. a silver cup

    b. a hunting horn

    c. a double-bladed scythe

    d. a sacred scroll of papyrus

19. In a certain vineyard near Timnah, Samson killed a lion with his bare hands and later found in its carcass _____.

    a. a pride of cubs about to be born

    b. a swarm of bees and honey

    c. five sacks of meal

    d. a message from God on a scroll

20. The shape of Noah's ark was _____.

    a. oblong

    b. trapezoid

    c. triangular

    d. rectangular

21. The Exodus delivered _____Hebrews from Egypt.

    a. 5,000

    b. 30,000

    c. 100,000

    d. more than 500,000

22. The last of the five books of Moses, Deuteronomy, takes the form of _____.

    a. three farewell speeches by Moses

    b. lamentations for sorrows past and future

    c. prophecies concerning the future of God's chosen

    d. a long letter addressed to the promised Messiah

23. Which of these major Jewish holy days is *not* mentioned by name in the Old Testament?

    a. Rosh Hashanah

    b. Yom Kippur

    c. Purim

    d. Hanukkah

24. The number of years that elapse between the last book of the Old Testament and the first book of the New Testament is _____ .

   a. 7

   b. 70

   c. 163

   d. 436

25. How many pairs of every kind of fowl and clean beast were on board Noah's ark?

   a. two

   b. three

   c. seven

   d. twelve

26. Queen Esther, who saved her brethren from the murder decree issued in her husband the king's name, is commemorated by Jews every year with the holiday of _____ .

   a. Succoth

   b. Purim

   c. Tabernacles

   d. Rosh Hashanah

27. The language of Jesus was _____ .

   a. Latin

   b. Greek

   c. Hebrew

   d. Aramaic

28. The New Testament was written in _____.

   a. Latin

   b. Greek

   c. Hebrew

   d. Aramaic

29. Jesus was not an only child. His mother also gave birth to _____.

   a. three other sons

   b. four other sons and at least two daughters

   c. a daughter

   d. seven other children

30. The "missing years" in Jesus' life were between the ages of _____.

   a. 5 and 13

   b. 12 and 30

   c. 13 and 21

   d. 25 and 30

31. The only recorded recollection of Jesus' boyhood adventures concerns a _____.

   a. replica of Noah's ark that He built

   b. stoning by jealous playmates

   c. visit to the Temple of Jerusalem

   d. vision He received in the wilderness

32. The soldiers who nailed Jesus to the cross vied over possession of His _____.

   a. crown of thorns

   b. ring

   c. coat

   d. Torah

UNSCRAMBLING TWO BIBLICAL LISTS

Psalm 150 speaks of musical instruments used in worship. Unscramble the instruments, using the circled letters to spell out the opening and closing command of that psalm.

PRUTTEM   a. ◯ _ _ _ _ ◯ _

TRYLESPA   b. _ _ _ _ _ _ ◯ _ ◯

PHAR   c. ◯ _ _ ◯

LIMBRET   d. _ ◯ _ _ ◯ _ _

GRENDIST   e. ◯ _ _ _ _ _ ◯

MUNSTIRNE TS   _ _ _ _ ◯ _ _ ◯ _ _ _

SOGRAN   f. ◯ _ _ ◯ _ _

BLYCAMS   g. _ ◯ _ _ _ ◯ _

_ _ _ _ _ _ _ _ _ _ _ _ _ _ _ -.

Unscramble the spiritual gifts listed by the apostle Paul and use the circled letters to spell out the message in I Corinthians 12:4.

DOSWIM   a. _ _ ◯ _ _ ◯

GLEDWOKEN   b. _ _ _ _ _ _ _ _ ◯

ATHIF   c. ◯ _ _ _ _

12

L A G H I N E   d. _ _ _ _ O _ _

C R A M I L E S   e. _ _ _ O _ _ _ O

C H E R P O P Y   f. _ O _ O _ _ _ _

S T E N C R I N M E   g. _ _ O _ _ _ _ _ _ _ O
D

G O S T U N E   h. _ _ _ O _ _ _

E N T R A P O N I T   i. O _ _ _ _ _ _ _ O _ _ O _ _
E R I T

Now there are diversities of _ _ _ _ _ , but the _ _ _ _
_ _ _ _ _ _.

33. According to Luke, Jesus sent disciples out two by two
    into every place He was to go. How many disciples did
    he send?

    a. 6

    b. 12

    c. 40

    d. 70

34. How many times did Jesus say that Peter should forgive
    his brother's sinning against him?

    a. 70

    b. 244

    c. 490

    d. 770

35. Judas Iscariot agreed to betray Christ for _____ pieces of silver.

    a. 12

    b. 30

    c. 40

    d. 50

36. Alone on the island of Patmos, John encountered a number of spectacular visions in groups of seven. Which of the following was not among them?

    a. trumpets

    b. horses

    c. seals

    d. vials

37. Jesus wrote _____ of the 27 books of the New Testament.

    a. none

    b. one

    c. three

    d. eight

38. There is no mention of the Virgin Birth or the Sermon on the Mount in the Gospels according to _____ and _____.

    a. Mark

    b. Matthew

    c. Luke

    d. John

39. Predicting at the Passover meal that one of His 12 disciples would betray Him, Jesus handed Judas _____.

    a. a sop

    b. a glass of wine

    c. His sandals

    d. an olive branch

40. To enter the Kingdom of Heaven, Jesus said that it was necessary to become like _____.

    a. a sparrow

    b. a mustard seed

    c. an innocent ewe

    d. a little child

41. Jesus rode into Jerusalem for the last time on a colt over a carpet of _____.

    a. palm branches and clothing

    b. lily petals

    c. vines from grape and olive trees

    d. gold dust

42. The missionary Paul spent _____ years in a hired house in Rome preaching and teaching in that center of the civilized world.

    a. two

    b. three

    c. seven

    d. twelve

43. The lost sheep that returns to the fold causes more joy in heaven than _____.

   a. 99 that never strayed

   b. the burnt offering of a hundred lambs

   c. the blooming roses of Sharon

   d. a thousand prayers from the pious

44. For all the elegance of his raiment, King Solomon, in the eyes of Jesus, was not as well dressed as _____.

   a. the humblest of believers

   b. the lilies of the field

   c. the sweetest singing hummingbird

   d. the love of little children

WHO'S WHO: THE FAMOUS AND THE FORGOTTEN

I don't want to be the first man on earth.

(Answers to the puzzles in Chapter 2 can be found on pages 172–176.)

45. From out of the burning bush that miraculously was not consumed, the Lord spoke to _____.

    a. Noah

    b. Abraham

    c. Jacob

    d. Moses

46. Who cursed the day he was born and wished that it would return to eternal darkness?

    a. Jeremiah

    b. Job

    c. Adam

    d. Jacob

47. The first "stranger in a strange land" was _____.

    a. Adam

    b. Moses

    c. Lot

    d. Daniel

48. What towering Old Testament figure was the offspring of an incestuous relationship?

    a. Moses

    b. Abraham

    c. Noah

    d. Isaiah

49. On the eve of his return to Canaan, Jacob entered into an all-night wrestling match with _____.

    a. his father, Isaac

    b. his twin brother, Esau

    c. God

    d. his son, Reuben

50. Besides wisdom, Solomon was renowned for his
    _____.

    a. love

    b. prophecies and warnings

    c. material blessings

    d. revenge upon transgressors

51. The infatuated Boaz bought some land and with it came
    the widow whom he wanted to marry. Her name was
    _____.

    a. Naomi

    b. Ruth

    c. Orpah

    d. Jessica

52. The expression "the apple of his eye" generally desig-
    nates paternal affection. Who was the first apple of whose
    eye?

    a. Seth of Adam's

    b. David of Jesse's

    c. Isaac of Abraham's

    d. Jacob of the Lord's

53. Before marching around the walls of Jericho, Joshua took
    special pains to spare the household of _____.

    a. the trumpeter Philobus

    b. the harlot Rahab

    c. his secret love, Shaddad

    d. the stonemason Og

54. Upon Moses' death, leadership of the Israelites wandering in the desert passed to _____.

 a. Joshua

 b. Eleazar

 c. Aaron

 d. Jacob

55. Who was known as the "woman who looked back"?

 a. Leah

 b. Bathsheba

 c. Miriam

 d. Lot's wife

56. Who was the only woman to rule over Judah, the southern section of Israel?

 a. Esther

 b. Abigail

 c. Huldah

 d. Athaliah

57. _____composed 3,000 proverbs and 1,005 songs.

 a. Jesus

 b. Solomon

 c. Caleb

 d. Boaz

58. After he was rescued in the bulrushes by Pharaoh's daughter, Moses was nursed by _____.

 a. Zipporah

 b. Miriam

 c. Fatima

 d. his mother

59. "Jehosophat," a favorite oath of many a motion-picture cowboy, is derived from _____.

    a. one of Job's expressions of woe

    b. a war cry of the Maccabees

    c. the chant of Hebrew slaves building the pyramids

    d. the name of a praiseworthy king of Judah

60. The city of Jerusalem was first destroyed by the armies of _____.

    a. King Nebuchadnezzar of Babylon

    b. King Ashurbanipal of Assyria

    c. Hophni of the Hittites

    d. Claudius of Rome

61. The prophet Hosea married a prostitute, a union that led to nothing but trouble. Her name, living on in history, was _____.

    a. Bathsheba

    b. Gomer

    c. Rahab

    d. Dinah

62. To his chagrin, Jacob discovered that his father-in-law had switched brides on him. This new relative of his was _____.

    a. Esau

    b. Reuben

    c. Laban

    d. Ishmael

22

WHO'S WHO IN THE BOOK OF GENESIS (Part 1)

Match the 13 names below with their descriptions. If you find this too easy, continue with Part 2 for the more difficult list of their friends and relatives.

____	1. Sarah	a. dreamed of a ladder stretched to heaven
____	2. Methuselah	b. breathed a sigh of relief when his father sacrificed a ram instead
____	3. Benjamin	c. lost his birthright over a bowl of soup
____	4. Rebekah	d. 600-year-old carpenter who survived a mighty flood
____	5. Ham	e. lived to the ripe old age of 969
____	6. Esau	f. grew up in Ur and at age 75 moved to Canaan
____	7. Isaac	g. had the unfortunate address of Sodom
____	8. Noah	h. Joseph's younger brother who was nearly detained in Egypt for an alleged theft
____	9. Abraham	i. grew up in the wilderness because of Sarah's jealousy
____	10. Ishmael	j. was cursed because he stumbled across his father dead drunk and naked.
____	11. Jacob	k. bore a child at 90 years of age
____	12. Seth	l. offered Isaac's servant a drink and gained a husband
____	13. Lot	m. the third son of Adam and Eve

63. One of the Israeli spies who rejected the majority report of giants in the land of Canaan was _____.

a. Caleb

b. Gideon

c. Ezekiel

d. Micah

64. Melchizedek, a figure who appears in both the Old and New Testaments, was _____.

a. a Babylonian king

b. a high priest not of the tribe of Levi

c. an angel

d. a minor prophet who spoke of the coming Messiah

65. Who was the king to whom the handwriting on the wall appeared?

a. Belshazzar

b. Nebuchadnezzar

c. Darius

d. Jehosophat

66. The first person declared king in Israel was _____.

a. Abimelech

b. Saul

c. David

d. Samuel

WHO'S WHO IN THE BOOK OF GENESIS (Part 2)

_____ 1. Joseph

_____ 2. Enoch

_____ 3. Abimelech

_____ 4. Hagar

_____ 5. Ephraim

_____ 6. Dinah

_____ 7. Laban

_____ 8. Reuben

_____ 9. Potiphar

_____ 10. Judah

_____ 11. Melchizedek

_____ 12. Tamar

_____ 13. Keturah

a. king of Salem and priest of God

b. Jacob's oldest son who pleaded that Joseph's life be spared

c. Abraham's third wife, blessed with six sons

d. walked with God and never died

e. played the harlot and had twins by her father-in-law

f. almost had sex with Sarah thinking she was Abraham's sister

g. had three sons—Er, Onan, and Shelah—two of whom met untimely deaths

h. slave woman who bore Abraham a son

i. hoodwinked Jacob into marrying his older daughter first

j. his dream that his family would bow down to him put him on his brothers' hit list

k. received a better blessing from Jacob (Israel) than his older brother

l. Jacob's daughter whose brothers brutally avenged her rape

m. his wife tried to seduce Joseph but failed

67. Job's three "comforters" were Eliphaz, Bildad, and
_____.

    a. Zophar

    b. Lemuel

    c. Hilkiah

    d. Michri

68. Who supervised the rebuilding of Jerusalem after the
captivity in Babylon?

    a. Daniel

    b. Isaiah

    c. Herod

    d. Nehemiah

69. An angry Jesus cast out from the Temple of Jerusalem
_____.

    a. the worshippers of Baal

    b. the plotters of His death

    c. the money changers

    d. exploitative physicians and lawyers

70. Who accompanied the apostle Paul on missionary journeys among the Gentiles in Cyprus, Antioch, and else-
where in Asia Minor?

    a. Barnabas

    b. Peter

    c. Ananias

    d. Apollos

EIGHTEEN MISSING KINGS

The eighteen kings who ruled the northern kingdom of Israel are hidden in the lettergrid below—vertically, horizontally, and diagonally.

x	b	a	h	a	g	h	a	i	h	a	k	e	p	b
b	h	s	a	o	h	e	j	y	t	u	m	e	a	l
w	z	a	h	a	o	h	e	j	o	a	k	a	n	i
u	q	u	a	a	v	e	i	m	r	a	s	u	x	m
h	i	x	i	c	i	r	f	o	h	h	f	m	i	a
e	o	v	z	l	m	r	h	t	a	m	a	e	r	o
j	e	s	a	o	d	e	a	e	d	c	b	n	m	b
d	g	q	h	u	j	v	e	h	i	l	u	a	i	o
b	c	a	a	e	m	n	o	p	c	u	v	h	z	r
y	l	u	o	n	a	d	a	b	i	a	w	e	x	e
e	m	u	l	l	a	h	s	g	r	t	z	m	u	j

Ahab	Jehoash	Omri
Ahaziah	Jehoram	Pekah
Baasha	Jehu	Pekahiah
Elah	Jeroboam	Shallum
Hoshea	Menahem	Zachariah
Jehoahaz	Nadab	Zimri

71. The virgin Mary's cousin Elisabeth also gave birth to an illustrious son. He was named _____.

    a. Matthew

    b. John the Baptist

    c. Peter

    d. Saul

72. Who observed that the "poor will be with us always"?

    a. Jesus

    b. Nicodemus

    c. James

    d. Paul

73. Whom did Mary visit with the news that she was going to give birth to a son who would be called Jesus?

    a. her fiance, Joseph

    b. her cousin, Elisabeth

    c. the priest Zacharias

    d. King Herod's governor in Jerusalem

74. Among the witnesses to the crucifixion of Jesus were _____.

    a. His mother

    b. His father

    c. Herod

    d. Judas

75. To whom did Jesus first talk of being "born again" as a requisite for entering the Kingdom of God?

    a. Paul

    b. Nicodemus

    c. Thomas

    d. Philip

FAMOUS DATES

Couples in the Bible often found each other, or acted together, in memorable ways. Below are listed some of these famous "dates." Name the couple involved.

1. He won her by defeating a giant but had to do in 200 more men to seal the bargain. _____ and _____

2. Their relationship ended when he woke up with a haircut. _____ and _____

3. She watered his camels, and his servant proposed for him. _____ and _____

4. She slept at his feet after a party; in the morning they got engaged. _____ and _____

5. This couple shared many hobbies, including persecuting the prophet Elijah. _____ and _____

6. Mismatched from the start, he knew of her checkered past before the wedding. _____ and _____

7. They plotted together to withhold money from the church. _____ and _____

8. When he awoke to find her beside him, he knew they were made for each other. _____ and _____

9. He had his pick of anyone in the kingdom; she won out after a name change. _____ and _____

10. He didn't discover that they were married until the morning after the honeymoon started. _____ and _____

BIG THREES (True/False)

Starting with the Trinity, Scripture is full of people who did things in threes. Write *T* next to the statements below that are true about these famous trios and write *F* next to those that aren't.

_____ 1. Peter, James and John were Jesus' closest friends.

_____ 2. Shadrach, Meshach, and Abednego, saved from a fiery furnace, were originally named Hananiah, Mishael, and Azariah.

_____ 3. Muppim, Huppim, and Ard were the Bible's first musical group.

_____ 4. David, Uriah, and Bathsheba squabbled over who should be king.

_____ 5. Shem, Ham, and Jepath didn't need to know how to swim.

_____ 6. Abraham, Isaac, and Jacob were famous because they never married.

_____ 7. Jubal, Jabal, and Tubalcain were the Bible's first inventors.

_____ 8. Jacob, Rachel, and Leah were beloved by their father's families.

_____ 9. Mary, Martha, and Lazarus were three of Jesus' favorite hosts.

76. In His years of teaching, Jesus said that He had never encountered faith to equal that of _____.

   a. Mary Magdalene, who put aside her waywardness

   b. Lazarus, who returned from the dead

   c. the boy who fed the multitudes

   d. the Roman centurion whose sick servant He healed

77. Whom did John the Baptist greet at the River Jordan as a "generation of vipers"?

   a. Pharisees and Sadducees

   b. publicans and sinners

   c. Romans and Greeks

   d. moneychangers and alms-sellers

78. Two mourning disciples encountered a stranger on the road from Jerusalem to Emmaus and told him that Christ had been crucified three days earlier. The stranger was _____.

   a. Lazarus

   b. Saul of Tarsus

   c. the resurrected Jesus

   d. Nicodemus

79. Who had an "enlightening" experience on the road to Damascus?

   a. Ananias

   b. Cornelius

   c. Philip

   d. Saul

80. Who were the two apostles arrested and jailed by the Sadducees for swearing that Jesus had risen from the dead?

   a. Paul and Timothy

   b. Matthew and Mark

   c. Peter and John

   d. Barnabas and Silas

81. What influential Pharisee and secret admirer of Christ received permission from Pontius Pilate to take His body down from the cross for burial in a private garden?

    a. Barnabas

    b. Nicodemus

    c. Clopas of Bethlehem

    d. Joseph of Arimathaea

82. King Herod learned of the birth of the "King of the Jews" through _____.

    a. three wise men from the East

    b. the shepherds who visited the manger where Jesus had been born

    c. the laundress who washed the swaddling clothes

    d. a taunting angel

83. The Roman procurator Pontius Pilate offered to free one of two Jews awaiting crucifixion. He let the Jewish community decide who would die, and they chose Jesus instead of _____.

    a. Barabbas, a condemned murderer

    b. Elias, a thief

    c. Philip, the zealot

    d. Timotheus, a tax evader

84. One of the men who approved the stoning to death of Stephen was _____.

    a. Thomas

    b. Caiaphas

    c. Saul of Tarsus

    d. Matthias

85. Matthew's fitness as an apostle was questioned because
_____.

   a. he had been promiscuous in his youth

   b. he was a tax collector

   c. he was not circumcised

   d. he was a devoted family man

86. The "good Samaritan" stopped to help a man who had
been robbed, stripped, and badly injured on the road
from Jerusalem to Jericho. Two previous travelers who
had passed him by were _____.

   a. a rabbi and a temple aide

   b. a physician and a peddler

   c. a grain merchant and a herdsman

   d. the man's brother and their uncle

87. Jesus gave Simon the surname of Peter and bestowed
upon the brothers John and James the surname of Boa-
nerges, which means _____.

   a. the peacemakers

   b. the stilt walkers

   c. the sons of thunder

   d. the builders of faith

88. After his suicide, Judas Iscariot was succeeded as an
apostle by _____.

   a. Justus

   b. Silas

   c. Philemon

   d. Matthias

WHO'S WHO IN THE BOOK OF ACTS (Part 1)

Match the 13 names below with their descriptions. If these illustrious characters are easy to identify, continue with Part 2 for the list of their more obscure friends and foes.

_____ 1. Ananias

_____ 2. Stephen

_____ 3. Philip

_____ 4. Barnabas

_____ 5. Cornelius

_____ 6. Simon

_____ 7. Aquila

_____ 8. Gamaliel

_____ 9. Silas

_____ 10. Lydia

_____ 11. Agrippa

_____ 12. Annas

_____ 13. Dorcas

a. gave up his magic act after being converted through Philip

b. part of the first jailhouse duet— a hit in Philippi

c. a missionary sidekick of Paul's who later had a falling out with him

d. a woman from Joppa whom Peter raised from the dead

e. a Pharisee who convinced the Sanhedrin to reduce the apostles' punishment to a mere flogging

f. a Damascus believer instrumental in Paul's conversion

g. preached a great sermon that got him stoned to death

h. explained the Book of Isaiah to an Ethopian eunuch

i. a high priest of Jerusalem who hauled Peter and John in for questioning

j. a tentmaker from Corinth who had Paul as a houseguest

k. a centurion whose desire for baptism surprised even Peter

l. a dealer in purple cloth who responded to the preaching team of Paul and Silas

m. a king so impressed with Paul's preaching that he almost became a convert himself

WHO'S WHO IN THE BOOK OF ACTS (Part 2)

_____ 1. Felix

_____ 2. Damaris

_____ 3. Matthias

_____ 4. Eutychus

_____ 5. Rhoda

_____ 6. Sapphira

_____ 7. Jason

_____ 8. Sceva

_____ 9. Apollos

_____ 10. Sosthenes

_____ 11. Elymas

_____ 12. Publius

_____ 13. Agabus

a. chief official of Malta whose father was healed by Paul

b. warned Paul of certain imprisonment in Jerusalem

c. a sorcerer blinded by Paul

d. the first female believer in Athens

e. a synagogue ruler of Corinth beaten up by the Jews over Paul's case being thrown out of court

f. the governor who held Paul prisoner for two years yet was unable to prove him guilty

g. an eloquent Bible teacher with a large following in Corinth and Ephesus

h. a servant girl accused of being out of her mind when she insisted Peter was knocking at the door.

i. the apostle chosen to replace Judas Iscariot

j. nodded off during Paul's sermon and fell out the window

k. his hospitality in Thessalonica got him into hot water

l. had seven sons who failed in their attempt to get into the exorcism business

m. perpetuated her husband's scam to undervalue their sold property and keep a share of the profit

SHEPHERD, SCRIBE & OTHER BIBLICAL OCCUPATIONS

People are often identified by the job they keep. Match the biblical characters below to the occupations for which they were known.

____	1. Cornelius	a. prophet
____	2. Ezra	b. fisherman
____	3. David	c. tentmaker
____	4. Paul	d. carpenter
____	5. Uriah	e. captain of the guard
____	6. Amos	f. angel
____	7. Lazarus	g. judge
____	8. Matthew	h. priest
____	9. Deborah	i. soldier
____	10. Agabus	j. tax collector
____	11. Rahab	k. centurion
____	12. Hezekiah	l. midwife
____	13. Michael	m. cup bearer to the king
____	14. Potiphar	n. scribe
____	15. Esau	o. shepherd
____	16. Nehemiah	p. beggar
____	17. Shiphrah	q. king
____	18. Andrew	r. prostitute
____	19. Shebna	s. herdsman
____	20. Joseph, Mary's husband	t. hunter

PEOPLE IN THE BIBLE WHO WEPT

Match the person to the sorrowful occasion.

____ 1. The elders at Ephesus

____ 2. Mary Magdalene

____ 3. Hagar

____ 4. Jeremiah

____ 5. John

____ 6. A woman who was a sinner

____ 7. Abraham

____ 8. David

____ 9. Esther

____ 10. Jesus

____ 11. Paul

____ 12. Peter

____ 13. Jacob

____ 14. Isaiah

a. came to mourn for Sarah and to weep for her

b. said, "mine eye poureth out tears unto God"

c. stood without at the sepulchre weeping

d. prayed . . . weeping and casting himself down

e. and Jonathan kissed one another, and wept one with another

f. cried, "mine eyes do fail with tears"

g. sat over against Ishmael, and lifted up her voice, and wept

h. said, "I have been with you at all seasons, serving the Lord with all humility of mind, and with many tears"

i. wept much, because no man was found worthy to open and to read the book

j. turning unto them said, "Daughters of Jerusalem, weep not for me"

k. kissed Rachel, and lifted up his voice, and wept

l. said, "I will weep bitterly"

m. went out, and wept bitterly at the crowing of the cock

n. all wept sore, and fell on Paul's neck, and kissed him

37

_____ 15. Job

_____ 16. Ezra

o. fell down at the king's feet, and besought him with tears to put away the mischief of Haman

p. stood at Jesus' feet behind him weeping, and began to wash his feet with tears

DECISIONS THAT SHAPED HISTORY

David falls in love with a married woman.

(Answers to the puzzle in Chapter 3 can be found on pages 177–179.)

89. In the days when there was no king in Israel, _____.

    a. there was no levy made

    b. every man did that which was right in his own eyes

    c. no man held respect for his neighbor

    d. Egypt maintained a reign of terror over the people

90. After conquering Jericho, the Israelites confidently marched on the tiny town of Ai and were soundly thrashed. Why?

    a. Someone had hoarded booty from the victory at Jericho.

    b. Unlike Jericho, Ai straddled a mountaintop.

    c. Israel had disobeyed God's command to spare Ai.

    d. Israel had turned to the Canaanite gods, thus incurring the Lord's wrath.

91. Gideon put out a fleece to see if _____.

    a. water condensed in the morning

    b. he should marry Jotham

    c. God would deliver Israel through him

    d. he should be made king

92. How did Saul meet Samuel and so become king?

    a. Saul was looking for his father's livestock.

    b. Saul went to Jerusalem to find a wife.

    c. Saul saw a vision of Samuel holding a crown.

    d. The Lord told Saul to find Samuel.

93. Joseph's famous coat of many colors signified
    _____.

    a. his desire to woo a noble woman

    b. that his father preferred him over his siblings

    c. his artistic temperament

    d. his need to stand out in the crowd

94. Moses was so angered at seeing Aaron's sculpture of the golden calf that he smashed to pieces the two tablets bearing the ten commandments written with the finger of God. After then destroying the calf, he _____.

    a. went back to the Lord for a duplicate set of the tablets

    b. cursed the followers of Aaron, withholding from them any further commandments

    c. sacrificed one of his sons

    d. went into the desert and did penance for two years

95. Exiled in Babylon, the Jews remained faithful to their own laws by _____.

    a. turning to the East when they said their silent prayers

    b. asking for vegetables and water instead of the meat and wine they were provided

    c. fasting on the Sabbath

    d. vowing to remain celibate until they were released

96. Impressed with God's intervention to protect Daniel in the lions' den, King Darius _____.

    a. converted to Judaism

    b. increased Daniel's holdings in the Medean Empire

    c. asked Daniel to decipher his troubling dreams

    d. had Daniel's accusers thrown into the den

97. The first instance of espionage was _____.

    a. Joseph's descent into Egypt

    b. Cain's residence in Nod

    c. Joshua's infiltration of Canaan

    d. Jacob's ladder

98. Mass extermination of Jews was not an original idea with Hitler and Germany's Third Reich. A previous proposal of a "final solution" for the so-called "Jewish problem" was made by _____.

    a. Potiphar to Pharaoh of Egypt

    b. Haman to King Ahasuerus of Persia

    c. one of the seven Palestinian rulers called Herod

    d. Nebuchadnezzar of Babylon

99. Jacob became a bigamist because _____.

    a. his first wife was barren

    b. he felt duty bound to marry his sister-in-law, who was carrying his child

    c. he had been promised Rachel if he would first marry Leah and give her seven sons

    d. he was tricked into marrying his first wife, who was not the woman he loved

100. Queen Esther did not tell her husband, Ahasuerus, the king of the Persians that she _____.

    a. had committed adultery twice

    b. was Jewish

    c. had been arrested for thievery

    d. was barren

101. One of King David's first acts after entering Jerusalem was to _____.

    a. move the ark of the covenant out of the house of Abinadab and into the grand new tabernacle in Jerusalem

    b. banish all Philistines from the kingdom

    c. dedicate a temple in memory of his good friend Jonathan, who had been slain in battle with the Philistines

    d. order that all families must tithe

102. Through his magnanimous spirit, Emperor Cyrus set free the Jews in Babylon _____.

    a. to spare them the famine

    b. to defuse the disreputable image of Babylon

    c. to spread the word of his benevolent reign

    d. to rebuild the temple in Jerusalem

103. Of his twin sons, Isaac preferred Esau to Jacob because _____.

    a. Esau had a more cheerful disposition

    b. he enjoyed eating Esau's game

    c. he thought Esau's hairiness was a sign of great strength

    d. Esau kept protesting his love for his father

DECISIONS, DECISIONS

Match the decision with the person who made it.

       I decided to . . .

____   1. look back   a. Martha

____	2. make a trade for thirty pieces of silver	b. Joseph
____	3. build a calf of gold to appease the Israelites	c. Matthew
____	4. not to prophesy in Nineveh	d. Esther
____	5. do housework rather than listen to Jesus teach	e. Achan
____	6. go before the king to save the Jews from Haman's persecution	f. Aaron
____	7. raise the baby found in the basket	g. Ruth
____	8. seek council from the witch of Endor	h. Mary
____	9. kill all royal males in Judah so I could rule myself	i. Hosea
____	10. divorce, and then remarry, Gomer	j. Jonah
____	11. refuse to eat the king's choice food	k. Saul
____	12. give up tax collecting to follow Jesus	l. Athaliah
____	13. have John the Baptist killed	m. Herod
____	14. keep the spoils earmarked for God	n. Joanna
____	15. stay with Naomi rather than return to my own people	o. Paul
____	16. anoint Jesus' feet with expensive ointment	p. Lot's wife
____	17. remain in my prison cell after an earthquake opened it.	q. Pharaoh's daughter
____	18. set the Syrians free after I defeated them by praying that God would blind them	r. Daniel
____	19. invite my family to come and live in Egypt	s. Judas
____	20. follow Jesus, supporting his ministry, after he healed me	t. Elisha

EXIT, STAGE RIGHT

Many people in the Bible were known for their dramatic exits. Match the exitees with their port of departure and means of escape.

PERSON	PORT OF DEPARTURE	MEANS OF ESCAPE
_____ 1. Paul (Saul)	a. outside Jerusalem	i. let down by a cord out a window
_____ 2. Jonah	b. Garden of Gethsemane	ii. driven out by God
_____ 3. Lot	c. Damascus	iii. took a chariot to heaven
_____ 4. Adam and Eve	d. Dagon's temple in Gaza	iv. ran away naked
_____ 5. Jesus	e. a west-bound boat	v. in a hail of stones
_____ 6. Elijah	f. Canaan	vi. in a basket
_____ 7. Samson	g. Sodom	vii. walking through a sea
_____ 8. Stephen	h. Jericho	viii. by taking more than 3,000 spectators with him
_____ 9. Israelites	i. Olivet	ix. went by a great fish

46

_____ _____ 10. Joseph   j. Egypt   x. on foot in
the dawn
one step
ahead of
brimstone

_____ _____ 11. Joshua's   k. Garden of   xi. in a caravan
spies   Eden

_____ _____ 12. A young   l. bank of the   xii. by a cloud,
man   river Jordan   which he
was taken
up into

104. Two women, each claiming to be the mother of the same baby boy, asked Solomon to resolve their dispute. He proposed to _____.

   a. chop the infant in half

   b. adopt him as his own son

   c. give each woman a trial period of mothering

   d. determine which woman loved God the more

105. At God's instruction, Noah made the ark with _____.

   a. Sinai sand

   b. cedars from Lebanon

   c. stone from the quarries of Mesopotamia

   d. gopher wood

106. Joseph married the virgin Mary _____.

   a. to stop any unpleasant gossip

   b. to avoid excess taxation

   c. to avoid conscription

   d. in obedience to an angel

107. When His friends learned that Jesus was exorcising evil spirits, they _____.

    a. sought to restrain Him for fear He was insane

    b. disassociated themselves from Him and the disciples

    c. became envious and spiteful

    d. sent the dregs of society to His door

108. Why did Joseph and Mary travel from Nazareth to Bethlehem?

    a. God wanted the Messiah to be born under a bright star.

    b. Three wise men had predicted bad omens for Nazareth.

    c. Joseph had to register with the tax collectors.

    d. Bethlehem had the most devout midwife in Judea.

109. On the road to Gaza, Philip encountered an Ethiopian eunuch who was reading the book of Isaiah while traveling in his splendid carriage. Listening to Philip's interpretations of certain passages, he asked _____.

    a. how Philip could believe in such fantastic things

    b. to be baptized

    c. Philip to teach in Africa

    d. if Jesus could restore his manhood should he be a believer?

110. In John's gospel, Jesus wept _____.

    a. at Judas Iscariot's treachery

    b. at the death of Lazarus

    c. because His parents made Him leave the temple

    d. at the beheading of John the Baptist

111. A pious man who had kept all the commandments from his youth was told by Jesus that he would have the eternal life he was seeking if he sold his worldly goods and gave to the poor. The man _____.

   a. immediately sold everything and turned over all his moneys to the needy

   b. became ecstatic at the prospect

   c. became sad and grievous

   d. was arrested by Roman guards for tax evasion

112. Before Pilate handed Jesus over to the soldiers for crucifixion, he had Him _____.

   a. bled

   b. bathed

   c. crowned with thorns

   d. whipped

113. Why did Jesus choose to eat and drink with disreputable people?

   a. He was seeking 12 men who would preach for Him.

   b. He had always depended on the kindness of strangers.

   c. He would become a better leader if He were acquainted with people from all walks of life.

   d. The sinners were more in need of His help than the righteous.

114. On learning that the infant Jesus had escaped his net, the enraged King Herod _____.

   a. ordered that Bethlehem be burned to the ground

   b. sent covert assassins in search of Jesus

   c. ordered every child in the land two years of age and under to be slain

   d. confiscated the property of the families of Joseph and Mary

115. Judas Iscariot told the Roman soldiers and temple police sent to arrest Jesus in the Garden of Gethsemane that he would identify their man by _____.

a. saying, "Speak to me, master"

b. passing in front of Him three times

c. offering Him a candle

d. kissing Him

116. After Jesus was taken away to be tried, Judas Iscariot, in remorse _____.

a. pleaded for forgiveness

b. fled to Rome

c. returned the money and committed suicide

d. became a wandering evangelist

117. Before the Last Supper, Jesus washed the feet of each of His disciples to teach the lesson of _____.

a. the persecutions to come

b. putting cleanliness next to Godliness

c. serving others before oneself

d. accompanying prayers with ritual

118. What did the chief priests and elders do with the 30 pieces of silver that Judas returned to them?

a. They bought a potter's field to bury strangers in.

b. They gave the money to Jesus' devoted follower Mary Magdalene.

c. They consecrated an olive orchard in the name of Judas.

d. They deposited the money in the treasury of the temple.

119. Jesus was tried by the chief priests and elders in Jerusalem for the crime of _____.

a. being an impostor

b. blasphemy

c. continually breaking the Sabbath rules

d. slander

120. Pontius Pilate, who would have been willing to free Jesus, dipped his hands in water to signify that _____.

a. the Jews henceforth should settle their own disputes

b. the wounds of Jesus would soon be washed and healed

c. the Jewish community should try to wash this sin from their conscience

d. he was not to be held accountable

121. Threatened with shipwreck en route from Crete to Rome, Paul persuaded his fellow passengers to _____.

a. fast and pray to Jesus for deliverance from catastrophe

b. cast lots to decide who should be tossed into the sea to lighten the load

c. throw their foodstuffs overboard so that the ship could ride higher

d. renounce their archaic religions and take up Christianity

A HARMONY OF THE GOSPELS

The life of Jesus is recorded by four gospel writers. Each emphasized different events in His life. Match the event on the left with the gospels in which it is recorded.

Clue: eight events appear once; three appear twice; six appear three times; and three appear four times.

	MATT.	MARK	LUKE	JOHN
1. The angels announce the birth of Jesus to the shepherds.				
2. The wise men visit Jesus.				
3. Jesus is baptized by John the Baptist.				
4. Jesus is tempted in the wilderness.				
5. The Lord's prayer is first taught.				
6. Nicodemus visits Jesus at night.				
7. The Samaritan woman meets the Messiah.				
8. Jesus feeds the 5,000.				
9. Jesus shocks the disciples by walking on water.				

10. The transfiguration reveals Christ's glory.			
11. The parable of the good Samaritan is taught.			
12. The rich young ruler seeks salvation.			
13. Lazarus is raised from the dead.			
14. Jesus teaches the two great commandments.			
15. Zacchaeus gets an unexpected house guest.			
16. Jesus makes a triumphant entry into Jerusalem.			
17. The parable of the ten virgins is taught.			
18. The Lord's supper is instituted.			
19. Jesus is crucified.			
20. The resurrected Jesus appears to two disciples on a road.			

MEMORABLE COMMENTS

The animals went in two by two.

(Answers to puzzles in Chapter 4 can be found on pages 180–182.)

122. The first recorded cover-up in history is by Cain in response to God's inquiry as to Abel's whereabouts. Guiltily, he replied,

a. "My brother is out working in the field, is he not?"

b. "Am I my brother's keeper?"

c. "Abel has always been shy. How mayest thy servant serve thee?"

d. "Lord, why come to me? Dost thou not see all things?"

123. Goliath, in watching David approach with slingshot in hand, bellowed out,

a. "O men of Israel, are ye so afraid that ye send a mere lad to fight?"

b. "My boy, if thou art looking for lost sheep, thou hast come to the wrong place."

c. "Come to me, and I will give thy flesh to the fowls of the air."

d. "Thou fool, if thou hast come to mock me, then even your god cannot protect thee."

124. Balaam, on his way back to Moab to lay a curse on Israel, found his faithful ass balking at going another step. After Balaam beat the animal three times, the ass spoke,

a. "Dost thou not see the angel blocking the way ahead?"

b. "Beat me but once more and the Lord shall strike thee dead."

c. "What have I done to thee that thou hast struck me these three times?"

d. "Wouldst thou rather ride a camel?"

IDENTIFY THAT FAMOUS QUOTE

Match the familiar verse with the book from which it comes.

_____ 1. I can do all things through Christ which strengtheneth me.

_____ 2. To every thing there is a season, and a time to every purpose under the heaven.

_____ 3. Seek ye first the kingdom of God, and his righteousness; and all these things shall be added unto you.

_____ 4. Call unto me, and I will answer thee, and shew thee great and mighty things, which thou knowest not.

_____ 5. Let every man be swift to hear, slow to speak, slow to wrath.

_____ 6. Dust thou art, and unto dust shalt thou return.

_____ 7. If we confess our sins, he is faithful and just to forgive us our sins.

_____ 8. Trust in the Lord with all thine heart; and lean not unto thine own understanding.

_____ 9. For the wages of sin is death; but the gift of God is eternal life through Jesus Christ our Lord.

a. Jeremiah

b. Hebrews

c. Genesis

d. Ezekiel

e. Proverbs

f. Romans

g. John

h. Philippians

i. Acts

58

_____ 10. Now faith is the substance of things hoped for, the evidence of things not seen.

_____ 11. Greater love hath no man than this, that a man lay down his life for his friends.

_____ 12. Behold, I stand at the door, and knock: if any man hear my voice, and open the door, I will come in to him.

_____ 13. The heavens declare the glory of God; and the firmament sheweth is handywork.

_____ 14. Believe on the Lord Jesus Christ, and thou shalt be saved.

_____ 15. Prophesy upon these bones, and say unto them, O ye dry bones, hear the word of the Lord.

j. Ecclesiastes

k. James

l. Matthew

m. I John

n. Revelation

o. Psalms

125. Moses, while watching the flock of his father-in-law, Jethro, came upon a burning bush from which a voice called out,

a. "Draw not nigh hither. Put off thy shoes from off thy feet."

b. "This is the day of the Lord. Into thy hands have I delivered the enemy."

c. "Go get thy brother Aaron."

d. "Thou shalt have no other gods before me."

126. "I the Lord thy God am a _____God, visiting the iniquity of the fathers upon the children unto the third and fourth generation of them that hate me."

    a. jealous

    b. holy

    c. righteous

    d. just

127. In a drunken revelry, King Belshazzar saw the handwriting on the wall, which said _____.

    a. "You are finished and your kingdom is divided."

    b. "Put away the wine or perish."

    c. "The days of your adversaries are numbered."

    d. "Jerusalem is yours for the taking."

128. To whom did Ruth say, "Whither thou goest, I will go"?

    a. the Lord

    b. her husband

    c. her mother-in-law

    d. her sister

129. In the words of _____, "It is not good that the man should be alone."

    a. Moses

    b. Mary Magdalene

    c. Adam

    d. the Lord God

130. When his son was killed, David said, "O my son Absalom, my son, my son Absalom! _____"

   a. Wherefore art thou O Absalom?

   b. I would have given thee ten shekels of silver and a girdle.

   c. Thou art the shame of my loins.

   d. Would God I had died for thee.

131. Long before the planet Earth became a global village, it was Solomon who observed, "As cold waters to a thirsty soul, so is _____"

   a. a letter from a distant lover

   b. good news from a far country

   c. honor from a monarch

   d. the clasp of friendship

132. "A fool's _____is his destruction."

   a. purse

   b. mouth

   c. pride

   d. greed

133. In a prayer to God, the prophet Jeremiah swore that "Thy words were found, and I _____."

   a. broadcast them near and far

   b. wrapped them about me like a silken robe

   c. did eat them

   d. cherish them to my marrow

I WISH I'D SAID THAT!

The Bible is filled with famous quotations that have become part of everyday speech. Below are ten such sayings. Can you remember who made the famous statement and to whom he or she was speaking?

QUOTATION	WHO SAID IT	TO WHOM
1. Bone of my bones, and flesh of my flesh.	_____	_____
2. I AM THAT I AM.	_____	_____
3. The Lord bless thee, and keep thee; the Lord make his face shine upon thee, and be gracious unto thee: The Lord lift up his countenance upon thee, and give thee peace.	_____	_____
4. The Philistines be upon thee.	_____	_____
5. Whither thou goest, I will go; and where thou lodgest, I will lodge: thy people shall be my people, and thy God my God.	_____	_____

6. Thy love to me
   was wonderful,
   passing the love
   of women.

   —————————— ——————————

7. Divide the living
   child in two, and
   give half to the
   one, and half to
   the other.

   —————————— ——————————

8. The Lord gave,
   and the Lord
   hath taken away;
   blessed be the
   name of the
   Lord.

   —————————— ——————————

9. Give me here
   John Baptist's
   head on a
   charger.

   —————————— ——————————

10. Get thee behind
    me, Satan.

   —————————— ——————————

134. After a fast of 40 days, Jesus was challenged by the
     Devil to turn stones into bread, to which He replied,

    a. "It is not the will of the Lord that I make a miracle
        to feed myself."

    b. "It is written that man shall not live by bread alone."

    c. "Get thee behind me, Satan."

    d. "Darest thou blaspheme the Lord by breaking bread
        with His anointed?"

135. "In my father's house are many mansions: _____."

    a. See that ye are fit to enter the humblest of them.

    b. In them shall dwell all of God's true children.

    c. I go to prepare a place for you.

    d. Blessed are those who shall know their splendor.

THE LORD'S PRAYER

The familiar words of the Lord's prayer are hidden in the criss-cross puzzle. Below the puzzle is the Lord's prayer, which you should fill in first to determine the words needed to complete the puzzle.

Our _____which art in _____,
_____be _____ _____. Thy
_____ _____.
Thy ____be _____on _____, as it is in heaven.
_____us this _____our _____ _____.
And _____us our _____, as we forgive our
_____. And _____us _____into _____,
but _____us from _____: For _____is
the kingdom, and the _____, and the _____,
for ever. Amen.

THE LAST SEVEN SAYINGS OF JESUS ON THE CROSS

Fill in the blanks.

1. Then said Jesus, Father, _____ _____;
   for they know_____ _____
   _____ _____.

2. Jesus said unto the (thief on the cross), Verily I say unto
   thee, _____shalt thou be with me _____
   _____.

3. He saith unto his mother, Woman, _____
   _____ _____! Then saith he to the
   disciple, _____ _____ _____!

4. Jesus cried with a loud voice, saying, Eloi, Eloi, lama
   sabachthani? Which is, being interpreted, My God, my God,
   why hast _____ _____ _____?

5. Jesus . . . saith, I _____.

6. Jesus . . . said, It _____ _____.

7. And when Jesus had cried with a loud voice, he said, Father,
   _____ _____ _____ I
   commend my _____: and having said thus, he
   gave up the ghost.

136. On being told that Jesus of Nazareth was the Messiah, Nathanael replied,

    a. "How soon may I touch Him?"

    b. "I am not worthy to be in His presence."

    c. "The day of salvation is nigh!"

    d. "Can there any good thing come out of Nazareth?"

137. One of the two thieves being crucified with Jesus said to Him,

    a. "Lord, remember me when Thou comest into Thy kingdom."

    b. "Lord, have mercy on me, a sinner."

    c. "Lord, art Thou indeed the Holy One of Israel?"

    d. "Lord, I am not worthy to hang with Thee, a saint."

138. At a marriage in Cana, Jesus said to His mother,

    a. "The occasion merits that there should be wine."

    b. "I did not expect to see thee here."

    c. "Woman, what have I to do with thee?"

    d. "This man and this woman will be blessed with great increase."

139. Jesus said that it was harder for a rich man to enter into the kingdom of God than for _____.

    a. a child to carry 1,000 tares on his back

    b. a harlot to regain her chastity

    c. a mule to become as wise as Solomon

    d. a camel to go through the eye of a needle

140. "Whosoever hateth his brother is a murderer: and ye know _____."

   a. that no murderer hath eternal life abiding in him

   b. that vengeance belongs to God alone

   c. another's hatred will rise up to smite you

   d. that hatred is the poison that separates you from God

141. Jesus valued the widow's mite over the contributions of the rich because _____.

   a. hers were untainted farthings

   b. she gave as a true believer

   c. she gave from hardship, they from abundance

   d. the rich in their large contributions have already received their reward from men

142. As Christ hung on the cross, the doubters and the scoffers challenged Him, the worker of miracles, to save His own life. In response, He said,

   a. "This suffering have I chosen in order to do the work of My Father."

   b. "My suffering is to cleanse away your sins."

   c. "Woe unto you, you generation of vipers."

   d. Nothing

143. In the parable of the Pharisee and the publican, the self-righteous Pharisee thought that he was superior because _____.

   a. he kept all the commandments

   b. he looked at God when praying

   c. he put on his finery to enter the temple

   d. he fasted and tithed

144. Immediately after Jesus was baptized, a voice from Heaven said,

   a. "Go, all of my children, and do likewise."

   b. "This is my beloved Son, in whom I am well pleased."

   c. "This is the day of the Lord, hear ye Him.

   d. "My Son shall go before you as a lamp unto your feet."

145. Hebrew elders, eager to entangle Him in His talk, asked Jesus whether it was right to pay taxes to the Romans. He responded, in effect,

   a. "Give unto them that which is theirs."

   b. "I have not come with the sword, but in peace."

   c. "Do not discuss such matters with me."

   d. "Remember the parable of the sowers and the reapers."

146. It is impossible, Jesus said, to be a money-oriented servant of the Lord because _____.

   a. no man can serve two masters

   b. men of the cloth should take a vow of poverty

   c. money is a curse upon religion

   d. wealth leads preachers to become wolves in sheep's clothing

147. When Jesus forgave the sins of the woman who had washed His feet with tears and anointed them with expensive ointment, the other guests at the table grumbled,

   a. "Who is He to forgive sins?"

   b. "If she can be forgiven, who can not?"

   c. "He glories in consorting with the lowest."

   d. "She makes a mockery of Him."

148. Jesus said to the bedridden victim of palsy,

    a. "Believe in Me and thy disease shall pass."

    b. "Soon thou shalt be with my Father in Heaven."

    c. "Arise, take up thy bed, and go unto thine house."

    d. "Blessed are the stricken, for they shall taste the power of God."

149. "They toil not, neither do they spin."

    a. The peacocks of Paradise

    b. The snow-tipped mountains of Syria

    c. The lilies of the field

    d. The waters of Phoenicia

150. Jesus' cry upon the cross, "My God, my God, why hast thou forsaken me?" first appears in _____.

    a. Job

    b. Psalms

    c. Isaiah

    d. Matthew

151. On the way into the temple, Peter and John were confronted by a beggar looking for some loose change. Peter responded,

    a. "God helps those who help themselves."

    b. "Depart from us, do you not know it is the Sabbath?"

    c. "Repent and be baptized in the name of Jesus."

    d. "Silver and gold have I none; but such as I have give I thee."

THE QUOTABLE JESUS.

To whom did Jesus speak these famous words?

_____ 1. Man shall not live by bread alone.

a. Peter

_____ 2. Let no fruit grow on thee henceforward forever.

b. Judas Iscariot

_____ 3. Wistye not that I must be about my Father's business?

c. adulterous woman

_____ 4. Touch me not; for I am not yet ascended to my Father.

d. Pilate

_____ 5. That thou doest, do quickly.

e. the devil

_____ 6. My kingdom is not of the world.

f. a fig tree

_____ 7. Get thee behind me, Satan.

g. Mary and Joseph

_____ 8. I am the way, the truth, and the life.

h. Thomas

_____ 9. Sell whatsoever thou hast, and give to the poor.

i. Martha

_____ 10. Today shalt thou be with me in paradise.

j. Mary Magdalene

_____ 11. The Son of man is come to seek and to save that which was lost.

k. Samaritan woman

_____ 12. Ought not Christ to have suffered these things?

l. Nicodemus

_____ 13. Love thy neighbour as thyself.

m. rich young ruler

_____ 14. Except a man be born again, he cannot see the kingdom of God.

n. Philip

_____ 15. He that hath seen Me hath seen the Father.

_____ 16. I am the resurrection, and the life.

_____ 17. Blessed is he, whosoever shall not be offended in me.

_____ 18. Neither do I condemn thee: go, and sin no more.

_____ 19. Go thy way; thy faith hath made thee whole.

_____ 20. God is a Spirit: and they that worship him must worship him in spirit and in truth.

o. Zacchaeus

p. Cleopas and friend

q. thief on the cross

r. a Pharisee

s. John the Baptist's disciples

t. Bartimaeus

152. In His last days, Jesus described His relationship with His disciples in these words:

a. "I am the vine, ye are the branches."

b. "I am the gate, ye are the fence."

c. "I am the door, ye are the pathway."

d. "I am the foundation, ye are the stones."

153. In closing the book of Revelation, John prayed,

a. "Not my will, but thine be done."

b. "Even so, come, Lord Jesus."

c. "May thy kingdom be forever."

d. "Worthy art thou, O Lord, to receive glory."

154. Jesus, in explaining His use of parables to His audience, said, in effect, that they were _____.

   a. a device to challenge the keenness of His audience.

   b. a result of His natural bent for allegory.

   c. His way to avoid pontificating.

   d. based on a wish to disguise His underlying message.

155. Satan challenged Jesus to jump from the top of the temple, saying that God would surely send angels to break His fall. Jesus responded,

   a. "First go and show thy own miraculous power."

   b. "Get thee behind Me, Satan."

   c. "Thou shalt not tempt the Lord thy God."

   d. "Soon I shall be in a place much higher than this."

156. Old Simeon, holding the infant Jesus in his arms and recognizing Him as the Messiah, told Mary that _____.

   a. she must be the happiest person in the world

   b. a terrible pain would befall her

   c. this child must be her whole life

   d. she was not to reprove or discipline her son

72

157. In the Sermon on the Mount, Jesus said, "Whosoever looketh on a woman to lust after her _____."

a. is no better than a harlot in the streets

b. turns his mind away from God

c. should have a millstone hung around his neck

d. hath committed adultery in his heart

———— 5 ————
PROPHECIES AND PROMISES

Let there be peace on earth.

(Answers to the puzzles in Chapter 5 can be found on pages 183–185.)

UNSCRAMBLING ISAIAH'S PROPHECY

Isaiah 53 is one of the most eloquent passages of prophecy in the Bible. Complete verses 3 and 5 by filling in the appropriate words in the column on the right. Then unscramble the circled letters to identify the object of Isaiah's prophecy.

He is despised   a. _ _ ◯ _ _ _ _ _
and _____
of men; a man of   b. ◯ _ _ _ _ _ _
_____and
acquainted with   c. _ _ ◯ _ _
_____:....
he was _____,   d. _ _ _ _ _ ◯ _ _
and we
esteemed him   e. _ ◯ _ _ _ _ _ _ ◯ _ _ _ _ _
not. . . . he was
wounded for our

_____,
he was bruised   f. _ _ _ _ ◯ _ ◯ _ _ _
for our

_____:
the chastise-   g. _ _ _ ◯ _
ment of our

_____
was upon him;   h. _ _ _ _ _ ◯ _
and with his __

we are _____.   i. ◯ _ _ _ _ _

_ _ _ _   _ _ _ _ _

77

FIND THE 20 MISSING PROPHETS

The names of 20 prophets are hidden in the lettergrid below—
horizontally, vertically, and diagonally.

A	T	H	N	O	M	N	M	I	C	A	H
H	P	A	A	K	U	K	K	A	B	A	H
S	I	G	H	H	H	E	T	H	I	A	M
L	Z	G	T	A	A	R	O	N	I	J	A
E	E	A	A	J	N	N	A	A	O	H	I
O	C	I	N	I	D	H	S	S	L	S	H
J	H	T	K	L	P	I	H	O	A	N	C
H	A	I	M	E	R	E	J	M	A	H	A
S	R	H	Z	A	Z	R	U	A	E	O	L
T	I	S	A	H	T	E	L	I	S	H	A
D	A	N	I	E	L	H	A	H	O	J	M
A	H	A	I	D	A	B	O	P	H	T	A

Amos	Habakkuk	Joel	Nathan
Daniel	Haggai	Jonah	Obadiah
Elijah	Hosea	Malachi	Samuel
Elisha	Isaiah	Micah	Zechariah
Ezekiel	Jeremiah	Nahum	Zephaniah

BLESSED ARE...

Finish the nine Beatitudes recorded in Matthew's Gospel.

Blessed are...

_____ 1. the poor in spirit

_____ 2. those who mourn

_____ 3. the meek

_____ 4. those who hunger and thirst for righteousness

_____ 5. the merciful

_____ 6. the pure in heart

_____ 7. the peacemakers

_____ 8. those persecuted for righteousness sake

_____ 9. those whom men revile and persecute

a. for they shall be filled

b. for they shall see God

c. for they shall obtain mercy

d. for theirs is the kingdom of heaven

e. for their reward is great in heaven

f. for they shall be called the children of God

g. for they shall be comforted

h. for they shall inherit the earth

i. for theirs is the kingdom of heaven

158. Although Abraham and Sarah were childless into their old age, the Lord promised them descendants who would _____.

a. reflect great glory upon their names

b. be as numerous as the stars

c. enter into squabbles with one another and need God's arbitration

d. have the most abundant harvest in Canaan

END TIMES PROPHECIES

Test your knowledge of the end times prophecies by filling in the blanks. The verses below are from six books—Matthew, I and II Thessalonians, II Timothy, II Peter, and Revelation. The order of the verses has been endorsed by no theologian with a specialty in eschatology. (The end of a _____indicates the end of a word.)

1. In the last _____ _____ times shall come.
2. For nation shall rise against nation, and _____ _____ _____.
3. Ye shall hear of wars and _____ _____ _____.
4. The _____of the Lord so cometh as a _____ in the _____.
5. The day shall not come, except . . . that man of _____ _____ _____.
6. But of that _____and _____ knoweth no man, . . . but my _____only.
7. The Lord himself shall descend from _____ with a _____.
8. For as the _____cometh out of the east, . . . so shall also the _____of the _____ of man.
9. He shall send his angels with a great _____ of a _____.
10. The _____in Christ shall _____ _____.
11. We . . . shall be _____up together with them in the_____, to _____the _____.
12. After the tribulation of those days shall the _____ _____ _____.
13. We look for new _____and a new _____, wherein dwelleth _____.

80

14. The devil that deceived them was cast into the _____ of _____and _____.
15. And God shall wipe away all _____from their _____; and there shall be no more _____, neither _____, nor _____, neither shall there be any more _____: for the former things are _____ _____.

159. In the wake of the flood, God told Noah that henceforth the manifestation of His covenant with the earth would be _____.

   a. a rainbow

   b. a dove

   c. the change of seasons

   d. a full moon

160. God was so pleased that King Solomon had asked for wisdom so that he might help others that He rewarded him with _____.

   a. a library exceeding that of Alexandria

   b. wealth, respect, and a long life

   c. the death of his adversaries

   d. peace throughout his reign

161. The land that God promised the Hebrew slaves in Egypt was _____.

   a. Mesopotamia

   b. Phoenicia

   c. Canaan

   d. Sinai

81

162. "Armageddon" designates the future conflict between _____.

   a. God and man

   b. God and Satan

   c. warmongers and peacemakers

   d. believers and infidels

163. In the gospel according to Luke, the second coming of Christ is likened to _____.

   a. another Garden of Eden

   b. an eternal day without night

   c. the days of Noah and the destruction of Sodom

   d. the sun rising in the east

164. In Jesus' covenant with His followers, bread and wine symbolize _____.

   a. His humanity and divinity

   b. His corporeal and spiritual lives

   c. His body and blood

   d. His suffering and redemption

165. Jesus likened anyone who took notice of His teachings to _____.

   a. a blind person who becomes blessed with vision

   b. a man who builds his house on solid rock

   c. a rich man who gives away his wealth

   d. a man who disdains food or drink for the joys of contemplation

ISAIAH: A DOUBLE ACROSTIC

The double acrostic on the next few pages spells out a prophecy from Isaiah in the grid. Fill in the answers you might already know and put the letters in the corresponding numbered squares in the grid. If you are stumped for an answer, you can work backward from the grid, using the letters you have already filled in as clues. On the grid itself, the shaded squares indicate spaces between words.

A. Fear not, Abram, I am thy $\overline{57}$ $\overline{196}$ $\overline{32}$ $\overline{169}$ $\overline{116}$ $\overline{120}$, and thy
   exceeding great reward. (Gen. 15:1)

B. Neither shall thy name any more be called Abram, but thy
   name shall be Abraham; for a $\overline{153}$ $\overline{19}$ $\overline{217}$ $\overline{114}$ $\overline{86}$ $\overline{160}$ of many
   nations have I made thee. (Gen. 17:5)

C. In the selfsame day was $\overline{8}$ $\overline{204}$ $\overline{181}$ $\overline{129}$ $\overline{170}$ $\overline{23}$ $\overline{68}$ circumcised, and $\overline{38}$ $\overline{192}$ $\overline{162}$ $\overline{177}$ $\overline{59}$ $\overline{74}$ $\overline{34}$ his son. (Gen. 17:26)

D. And Reuben spake unto his father, saying, $\overline{142}$ $\overline{199}$ $\overline{213}$
   $\overline{191}$ $\overline{210}$ $\overline{63}$ two sons, if I bring him not to thee. (Gen. 42:37)

E. If (a man) smite out his manservant's $\overline{149}$ $\overline{53}$ $\overline{100}$ $\overline{13}$ $\overline{67}$,
   . . . he shall let him go free. (Exod. 21:27)

F. $\overline{45}$ $\overline{115}$ $\overline{110}$ $\overline{75}$ $\overline{220}$ $\overline{12}$ thou shalt give the more inheritance,
   and to few thou shalt give the less inheritance. (Num. 26:54)

G. Ye shall not go after $\overline{97}$ $\overline{70}$ $\overline{42}$ $\overline{182}$ $\overline{104}$ gods, of the gods of the people which are round about you. (Deut. 6:14)

H. Naomi said unto her two daughters $\overline{4}$ $\overline{188}$ $\overline{137}$ $\overline{37}$ $\overline{55}$, Go, return each to her mother's house. (Ruth 1:8)

I. He read therein before the street that was before the water gate from the morning until $\overline{101}$ $\overline{72}$ $\overline{29}$ $\overline{189}$ $\overline{155}$ $\overline{91}$. (Neh. 8:3)

J. When I lie down, I say, When shall I arise, and the night be gone? and I am full of $\overline{51}$ $\overline{132}$ $\overline{200}$ $\overline{17}$ $\overline{65}$ $\overline{147}$ $\overline{195}$ $\overline{108}$ to and fro unto the dawning of the day. (Job 7:4)

K. $\overline{99}$ $\overline{1}$ $\overline{85}$ $\overline{176}$ $\overline{130}$ $\overline{185}$ $\overline{96}$ $\overline{27}$ $\overline{141}$ by searching find out God? (Job 11:7)

L. The waters wear the stones: thou $\overline{135}$ $\overline{88}$ $\overline{212}$ $\overline{174}$ $\overline{69}$ $\overline{203}$ $\overline{180}$ away the things which grow out of the dust of the earth. (Job 14:19)

M. I am troubled; I am bowed down greatly; I $\overline{118}$ $\overline{47}$ $\overline{208}$ $\overline{103}$ $\overline{83}$ $\overline{36}$ $\overline{133}$ $\overline{136}$ $\overline{183}$ $\overline{61}$ all the day long. (Ps. 38:6)

N. For God is my King of old, working salvation in the midst of the earth. Thou $\overline{167}$ $\overline{30}$ $\overline{87}$ $\overline{39}$ $\overline{6}$ $\overline{3}$ $\overline{134}$ $\overline{215}$ $\overline{121}$ $\overline{94}$ $\overline{106}$ the sea by thy strength: thou brakest the heads of the dragons in the waters. (Ps. 74:12–13)

O. Let thy fountain be blessed: and rejoice with the wife of thy $\overline{211}$ $\overline{15}$ $\overline{98}$ $\overline{161}$ $\overline{52}$. (Prov. 5:18)

84

P. The father of a fool hath no __ __ __ . (Prov. 17:21)
   168 119 124

Q. But thou hast utterly rejected us; thou art very __ __ __
   89 62 159
   __ __ against us. (Lam. 5:22)
   139 50

R. Not every one that saith unto me, Lord, Lord, shall enter
   into the kingdom of heaven; but he that __ __ __ __ __
   117 25 78 95 186
   __ __ __ __ __ __ __ of my Father which is in
   143 46 163 64 202 214 127
   heaven. (Matt. 7:21)

S. Come unto me, all ye __ __ __ __ __ __ __ __ __
   109 71 126 58 26 90 112 219 54
   __ __ __ __ __ __ __ __ __ __ __ __ __ __
   79 92 2 146 11 166 40 7 44 198 172 178 138 187
   __ __ __ . (Matt. 11:28)
   157 151 60

T. Upon this rock I will __ __ __ __ __ my church. (Matt.
   150 48 80 33 10
   16:18)

U. And again he denied with an __ __ __ __ , I do not know
   148 173 9 18
   the man. (Matt. 26:72)

V. Why was this __ __ __ __ __ of the ointment made?
   31 152 179 21 43
   (Mark 14:4)

W. I am the __ __ __ __, ye are the branches. (John 15:5)
   128 175 73 209

X. There is therefore now no __ __ __ __ __ __ __ __
   206 201 76 107 197 123 145 56
   __ __ __ __ . (Rom. 8:1)
   82 218 171 194

Y. For I reckon that the __ __ __ __ __ __ __ __ __ __
   81 16 102 158 111 28 156 5 49 122
   of this present time are not worthy to be compared with
   the glory which shall be revealed in us. (Rom. 8:18)

Z. And withal they learn to be idle, . . . and not only idle, but
$\overline{41}$ $\overline{216}$ $\overline{66}$ $\overline{105}$ $\overline{20}$ $\overline{113}$ $\overline{84}$ $\overline{125}$ also and busybodies. (I Tim.
5:13)

AA. Paul, a $\overline{35}$ $\overline{140}$ $\overline{131}$ $\overline{22}$ $\overline{193}$ $\overline{93}$ $\overline{205}$ $\overline{154}$ of Jesus Christ. (Phi-
lem. 1)

BB. Who shall not fear thee, O Lord, and glorify thy name?
for thou only art $\overline{14}$ $\overline{207}$ $\overline{164}$ $\overline{24}$ (Rev. 15:4)

CC. When the thousand years are expired, Satan shall be loosed
out of his prison, and shall go out to deceive the nations
which are in the four quarters of the earth, Gog and
$\overline{190}$ $\overline{144}$ $\overline{77}$ $\overline{165}$ $\overline{184}$, to gather them together to battle. (Rev.
20:7–8)

✱ 1	S 2	N 3		H 4	Y 9		N 6	S 7	C 8	U ●		T 10	S 11
F 12		E 13	BB 14	O 15	Y 16		J 17	U 18	B 19	Z 20	V 21		AA 22
C 23	BB 24		R 25		S 26	K 27	Y 28	I 29		N 30		V 31	A 32
T 33	C 34		AA 35	M 36	H 37	C 38	N 39	S 40		Z 41	G 42	V 43	S 44
	F 45	R 46	M 47	T 48	Y 49	Q 50		J 51	O 52	E 53	S 54		H 55
X 56	A 57	S 58		C 59	S 60	M 61	Q 62	D 63		R 64	S 65	Z 66	E 67
	C 68	L 69		G 70	S 71	I 72	W 73	C 74		F 75	X 76	CC 77	R 78
S 79		T 80	Y 81		X 82	M 83	Z 84	K 85	B 86	N 87		L 88	Q 89
S 90	T 91		S 92	AA 93	N 94		R 95	K 96	G 97	O 98		K 99	E 100
I 101	Y 102	M 103	G 104	Z 105	N 106	X 107	J 108	S 109		F 110	Y 111		S 112
Z 113	B 114	P 115	A 116	R 117		M 118	P 119	A 120		N 121	Y 122		X 123
P 124		Z 125	S 126	R 127	W 128	C 129	K 130	AA 131	J 132	M 133		N 134	
L 135	M 136	H 137	S 138		Q 139	AA 140	K 141	D 142	R 143		CC 144	X 145	S 146
	J 147	U 148	E 149		T 150	S 151		V 152	B 153	AA 154	I 155	Y 156	S 157
	Y 158	Q 159	B 160		O 161	C 162	R 163		BB 164	CC 165	S 166	N 167	
P 168	A 169	C 170	X 171	S 172	U 173	L 174		W 175	K 176		C 177	S 178	
V 179	L 180	C 181	G 182	M 183	CC 184	K 185	R 186		S 187	H 188	I 189		CC 190
D 191		C 192	AA 193	X 194	J 195		A 196	X 197		S 198	D 199	J 200	X 201
	R 202	L 203		L 204	AA 205	X 206	BB 207	M 208	W 209		D 210	O 211	
L 212	D 213	R 214	N 215	Z 216	B 217	X 218	S 219	F 220					

87

COMMANDMENTS
AND CURSES

Why does she want tio give him a haircut?

(Answers to the puzzles in Chapter 6 can be found on pages 186–188.)

166. The Lord, testing Abraham, asked him to sacrifice his son Isaac by _____.

   a. making a burnt offering of him

   b. drowning him in the Nile

   c. throwing him off a pyramid

   d. abandoning him in the wilderness

167. At the Lord's behest, Moses built a fiery serpent of brass to _____.

   a. terrify the pursuing Egyptians

   b. expiate for the sins of Adam

   c. replace the golden calf

   d. heal snakebite

168. The rite of circumcision symbolizes _____.

   a. a covenant between God and man

   b. man's willingness to sacrifice his life for God

   c. mortification of the flesh

   d. man's becoming one with God through the letting of blood

169. Miriam criticized her brother Moses for marrying an Ethiopian woman and God for not speaking to her directly. As punishment she became _____.

   a. dumb

   b. leprous

   c. stricken with pox

   d. deprived of her lover

170. For poking fun at the prophet Elisha's baldness, 42 children were _____.

a. literally tongue-tied for 40 days

b. made to cleanse their mouths with bitter tablets of salt

c. torn by two she-bears

d. scalped

171. In Exodus, it is said that if your bull gored a slave, you had to pay the slave's owner _____.

a. another slave

b. 30 shekels of silver

c. all of your fertile fields

d. nothing; slaves were considered to be expendable

172. In reprisal for the building of the golden calf, Moses ordered

a. the murder of 3,000 idolators.

b. a fast of 40 days for all the children of Israel.

c. the amputation of the right hand of each of the artisans.

d. a year's vow of silence and penitence.

173. For having eaten fruit from the tree in the garden, God put a curse on Eve. He said that she would _____.

a. be returned to Adam's rib

b. experience pain in childbirth

c. never have dominion over men

d. be bitten by a snake

174. God destroyed Sodom and Gomorrah with fire and brimstone because _____.

a. of rampant homosexuality

b. of the unbelief of Lot and his wife

c. there were not ten righteous men in them

d. of Abraham's curse on the cities

175. Under the Mosaic law, if a man rapes an unbetrothed virgin, he shall _____.

   a. be forced to marry her

   b. be stoned

   c. be required to sacrifice a goat

   d. be cast into prison

176. Jewish law permitted a couple a "honeymoon" of _____.

   a. seven days

   b. forty days

   c. one year

   d. none of the above

177. Vomited onto the beach by an enormous fish, Jonah went to Nineveh to tell its citizens _____.

   a. they would be overthrown in 40 days

   b. the time of the Messiah was at hand

   c. a great tax would be levied to test their charity

   d. they would be receiving special honors from the Lord

178. The Talmud is _____.

   a. the Five Books of Moses

   b. the history of the Diaspora

   c. the log of Noah's odyssey

   d. the interpretation of the laws of Judaism

COMMANDMENTS FROM THE NEW TESTAMENT

Unscramble the following New Testament commandments.

1. Jesus told the Pharisee the two great commandments were to love the Lord with all thy

    R A H E T   a. _ _ _ _ _

    U S L O   b. _ _ _ _

    D I M N   c. _ _ _ _

and thy

    G R O U B E H I N   d. _ _ _ _ _ _ _ _ _

as

    F L Y S E T H   e. _ _ _ _ _ _

2. Paul told the Ephesians to put on the whole armor of God; gird your loins with

    T H U R T   a. _ _ _ _ _

put on the breastplate of

    S I T H E S O G R   b. _ _ _ _ _ _ _ _ _ _ _ _ _

    U E N S

shod feet with the

    S P O G L E F O   c. _ _ _ _ _ _ _ _ _ _ _ _ _

    A C E P E

take the shield of

    T H I F A   d. _ _ _ _ _

and the helmet of

    A S T O N I V A L   e. _ _ _ _ _ _ _ _ _

and the sword of the

    T R I P I S   f. _ _ _ _ _

3. Paul told Timothy to "let no man despise thy youth" but to be an example to believers in

    D R O W   a. _ _ _ _

    S T O N I V A C R   b. _ _ _ _ _ _ _ _ _ _ _

    O N E

T H I C A R Y   c. _ _ _ _ _ _ _

P I S T I R   d. _ _ _ _ _ _

A F H I T   e. _ _ _ _ _

U T R Y P I   f. _ _ _ _ _

4. Paul told the Philippians to think on the following things:
Whatsoever is . . .

R U T E   a. _ _ _ _

S H E T O N   b. _ _ _ _ _ _

S T U J   c. _ _ _ _

R U P E   d. _ _ _ _

O V Y L E L   e. _ _ _ _ _ _

D O G O T R E P O R   f. _ _ _ _ _ _ _ _ _

anything of

T R U V I E   g. _ _ _ _ _ _

S A P I R E   h. _ _ _ _ _ _

THE TEN COMMANDMENTS

Rearrange the Ten Commandments in the right order.

_____Thou shalt not kill.

_____Thou shalt not covet.

_____Thou shalt not take the name of the Lord thy God in
vain.

_____Remember the sabbath day, to keep it holy.

_____Thou shalt not commit adultery.

_____Thou shalt not make unto thee any graven image.

_____Honour thy father and thy mother.

_____Thou shalt have no other gods before me.

_____Thou shalt not bear false witness.

_____Thou shalt not steal.

THE WORKS OF THE FLESH AND THE FRUIT OF THE SPIRIT

In the lettergrid below are hidden the works of the flesh and the fruit of the spirit (Gal. 5:18–23). A little searching should locate them all. The words used in the list are compiled from several translations of the Bible, as the King James version uses terms that are now obscure, such as variance and emulations.

S	E	L	F	C	O	N	T	R	O	L	H	S	T	A
S	Y	S	U	O	L	A	E	J	P	D	S	P	F	H
E	H	S	S	E	R	E	G	N	A	E	R	A	A	S
N	T	E	N	V	Y	N	E	S	S	R	I	T	R	S
N	A	N	O	S	T	R	I	F	E	T	S	I	C	E
E	R	D	I	A	N	D	M	C	H	A	E	E	H	N
K	N	O	T	R	O	E	P	F	A	H	L	N	C	E
N	S	O	C	L	I	S	U	V	E	T	F	C	T	L
U	T	G	A	T	S	L	R	O	C	N	I	E	I	T
R	E	T	F	E	N	O	I	N	A	H	S	O	W	N
D	R	O	N	E	E	V	T	F	E	S	H	T	N	E
Y	R	T	S	E	S	E	Y	O	P	A	N	E	S	G
Y	S	S	E	N	S	U	O	I	T	N	E	C	I	L
C	O	S	T	K	I	N	D	N	E	S	S	H	A	T
A	N	J	E	O	D	C	A	R	O	U	S	I	N	G

FLESH		*SPIRIT*
anger	idolatry	faithfulness
carousing	impurity	gentleness
dissension	jealousy	goodness
drunkenness	licentiousness	joy
envy	selfishness	kindness
factions	strife	love
fornication	witchcraft	patience
hatred		peace
		self control

179. In the Old Testament, a man who finds "some unclean-ness" in his wife can write a bill of divorcement and send her out of the house, and both of them can remarry. In the New Testament, "What therefore God hath joined together, _____."

    a. shall be blessed of the Lord

    b. shall inherit the Kingdom of Heaven

    c. let not man put asunder

    d. let no earthly power condemn

180. Herod Antipas of Galilee violated the Judaic law and was reproved by John the Baptist for _____.

    a. wooing away Herodias, Herod's sister-in-law

    b. threatening to liberalize Sabbath regulations

    c. discouraging the practice of tithing

    d. putting money before the Messiah

181. Jesus declared that on two commandments hung "all the law and the prophets." One was "Thou shalt love the Lord thy God with all thy heart, and with all thy soul, and with all thy mind." The other was _____.

a. "Thou shalt do good unto them that hate you"

b. "By the sweat of thy brow shalt thou eat bread"

c. "Thou shalt do unto others as thou wouldst have them do unto you"

d. "Thou shalt love thy neighbor as thyself"

182. His critics said that Jesus had profaned the sabbath by _____.

a. prosletyzing for more followers

b. continuing without rest his journeys across the land

c. healing a man with a withered hand

d. taking the same food and drink as on all other days

183. In the Sermon on the Mount, Jesus advised that one should give to the needy _____.

a. cheerfully

b. abundantly

c. secretly

d. wisely

184. The demand that Jesus made of the twelve followers who would become apostles was _____.

a. that they put His life before their own

b. that they never deny or betray Him

c. chastity, sobriety, abstinence

d. that they forsake all possessions

A COMMANDMENT: A DOUBLE ACROSTIC

The double acrostic on the next few pages spells out a commandment of Jesus'. Fill in the answers you might already know and put the letters in the corresponding numbered squares in the grid. If you are stumped for an answer, you can work backward from the grid, using the letters you have already filled in as clues. On the grid itself, the shaded squares indicate spaces between words.

A. But of the $\overline{85}$ $\overline{19}$ $\overline{57}$ $\overline{124}$ $\overline{129}$ of the tree which is in the midst of the garden, God hath said, Ye shall not eat of it, neither shall ye touch it, lest ye die. (Gen. 3:3)

B. And she bare him a son, and he called his name Gershom: for he said, I have been a stranger in a $\overline{5}$ $\overline{108}$ $\overline{40}$ $\overline{66}$ $\overline{128}$ $\overline{93}$ $\overline{213}$ land. (Exod. 2:22)

C. And if a man have committed a sin worthy of death, and he be to be put to death, and thou $\overline{48}$ $\overline{193}$ $\overline{103}$ $\overline{24}$ him on a tree (Deut. 21:22)

D. And he shall be unto thee a restorer of thy life, and a nourisher of thine old age: for thy daughter in law, which $\overline{67}$ $\overline{3}$ $\overline{12}$ $\overline{173}$ $\overline{132}$ $\overline{21}$ thee, which is better to thee than seven sons, hath born him. (Ruth 4:15)

E. Then he said to Gehazi, Gird up $\overline{133}$ $\overline{65}$ $\overline{148}$ $\cdot$ $\overline{51}$ $\overline{99}$ $\overline{28}$ $\overline{191}$ $\overline{122}$, and take my staff in thine hand, and go thy way. (II Kings 4:29)

99

F. (Job) said, Naked came I out of my mother's womb, and
   naked   shall   I $\overline{94}$ $\overline{185}$ $\overline{169}$ $\overline{4}$ $\overline{209}$ $\overline{74}$ $\overline{82}$ $\overline{37}$ $\overline{121}$ $\overline{146}$ $\overline{138}$
   $\overline{13}$ $\overline{157}$: the Lord gave, and the Lord hath taken away; blessed
   be the name of the Lord. (Job 1:21)

G. More   to   be   desired   are $\overline{89}$ $\overline{197}$ $\overline{164}$ $\overline{71}$ $\overline{97}$ $\overline{134}$ $\overline{109}$ $\overline{182}$
   $\overline{152}$ $\overline{176}$ $\overline{195}$ $\overline{92}$, yea, than much fine gold: sweeter also than
   honey and the honeycomb. (Ps. 19:10)

H. Who is this King of glory? The Lord strong and mighty, the
   Lord mighty $\overline{63}$ $\overline{149}$ $\overline{154}$ $\overline{42}$ $\overline{214}$ $\overline{112}$ $\overline{199}$ $\overline{145}$. (Ps. 24:8)

I. I $\overline{175}$ $\overline{131}$ $\overline{10}$ $\overline{123}$ $\overline{32}$ $\overline{46}$ $\overline{166}$ $\overline{69}$ $\overline{127}$ $\overline{208}$ $\overline{105}$ $\overline{78}$ $\overline{91}$ $\overline{38}$
   $\overline{95}$ $\overline{54}$ $\overline{150}$ $\overline{88}$ $\overline{136}$ $\overline{60}$ $\overline{187}$ $\overline{25}$ $\overline{196}$ $\overline{15}$ $\overline{114}$ hills, from whence
   cometh my help. (Ps. 121:1)

J. They come from a far country, from the end of heaven,
   even the Lord, and the weapons of his indignation, to destroy
   the $\overline{201}$ $\overline{189}$ $\overline{130}$ $\overline{17}$ $\overline{106}$ $\overline{140}$ $\overline{181}$ $\overline{43}$ $\overline{120}$. (Isa. 13:5)

K. The Lord hath mingled to perverse spirit in the midst thereof:
   and they have caused Egypt to err in every work thereof,
   as a drunken man staggereth in his $\overline{144}$ $\overline{155}$ $\overline{101}$ $\overline{80}$ $\overline{64}$. (Isa.
   19:14)

L. The Lord is good unto them $\overline{14}$ $\overline{83}$ $\overline{200}$ $\overline{141}$ $\overline{45}$ $\overline{158}$ $\overline{73}$ $\overline{52}$
   for him, to the soul that seeketh him. (Lam. 3:25)

M. Who is he that saith, and it cometh to pass, when the Lord
   $\overline{98}$ $\overline{210}$ $\overline{184}$ $\overline{72}$ $\overline{90}$ $\overline{110}$ $\overline{26}$ $\overline{126}$ $\overline{205}$ $\overline{147}$ it not? (Lam. 3:37)

N. And of thy garments thou didst take, and deckedst thy high places with divers colours, and playedst the harlot thereupon: the like things shall not come, neither shall it be so. Thou hast also taken thy fair jewels of my gold and my silver, which I had given thee, and madest to thyself images of men, and ‾‾204‾ ‾151‾ ‾111‾ ‾115‾ ‾47‾ ‾177‾ ‾143‾ ‾100‾ ‾180‾ ‾86‾ ‾160‾ whoredom with them. (Ezek. 16:16–17)

O. But who may abide the day of his coming? and who ‾55‾ ‾6‾ ‾39‾ ‾33‾ ‾68‾ ‾215‾ ‾1‾ ‾190‾ ‾186‾ ‾61‾ when he appeareth? for he is like a refiner's fire, and like fullers' soap. (Mal. 3:2)

P. He shall give his angels charge concerning thee: and in their hands they shall bear thee up, lest at any time thou ‾183‾ ‾59‾ ‾137‾ ‾77‾ thy foot against a stone. (Matt. 4:6)

Q. Our father which are in heaven, ‾161‾ ‾96‾ ‾58‾ ‾142‾ ‾167‾ ‾62‾ ‾198‾ ‾20‾ be thy name. (Matt. 6:9)

R. ‾27‾ ‾212‾ ‾118‾ ‾153‾ ‾49‾ ‾21‾ ‾113‾ ‾171‾ ‾102‾ ‾87‾ ‾79‾ to hear, let him hear. (Matt. 13:9)

S. So then after the Lord had spoken unto them, he was received up into heaven, and sat on the right ‾35‾ ‾7‾ ‾119‾ ‾44‾ of ‾192‾ ‾11‾ ‾104‾ . (Mark 16:19)

T. He ‾53‾ ‾139‾ ‾29‾ ‾170‾ ‾70‾ ‾178‾ ‾165‾ ‾211‾ ‾16‾ ‾107‾ his servant Israel, in remembrance of his mercy. (Luke 1:54)

101

U. The night is far spent, the day is at hand: let us therefore $\overline{117}$ $\overline{31}$ $\overline{81}$ $\overline{9}$ off the works of darkness, and let us put on the armour of light. (Rom. 13:12)

V. That we may lead a quiet and peaceable life in all godliness and $\overline{206}$ $\overline{18}$ $\overline{168}$ $\overline{84}$ $\overline{188}$ $\overline{174}$ $\overline{36}$. (I Tim. 2:2)

W. So also Christ glorified not himself to be made an high priest; but he that said unto him, Thou art my Son, $\overline{34}$ $\overline{56}$ $\overline{75}$ $\overline{202}$ $\overline{162}$ have I begotten thee. (Heb. 5:5)

X. How that they told you there should be mockers in the last time, who should walk after their own ungodly $\overline{8}$ $\overline{156}$ $\overline{159}$ $\overline{41}$ $\overline{172}$. (Jude 18)

Y. I am he that liveth and was dead; and, behold, I am alive for evermore, Amen; and have the $\overline{125}$ $\overline{207}$ $\overline{23}$ $\overline{163}$ of $\overline{2}$ $\overline{116}$ $\overline{30}$ $\overline{194}$ and of death. (Rev. 1:18)

Z. And the four angels were loosed, which were prepared for an hour, and a day, and a $\overline{179}$ $\overline{135}$ $\overline{203}$ $\overline{76}$ $\overline{30}$, and a year, for to slay the third pard of men. (Rev. 9:15)

A crostic puzzle grid:

1 O	2 Y	3 D	4 F	■	5 B	6 O	7 S	8 X	9 W	■	10 I	11 S	12 D
13 F	■	14 L	15 I	16 T	■	17 J	18 V	19 A	20 Q	■	21 R	22 D	23 Y
■	24 C	25 I	26 M	■	27 R	28 E	29 T	30 Z	■	31 U	32 I	33 O	
34 W	35 S	36 V	■	37 F	38 I	39 O	40 B	41 X	■	42 H	43 J	44 S	
45 L	46 I	47 N	48 C	■	49 R	50 Y	51 E	■	52 L	53 T	54 I	■	55 O
56 W	57 A	58 Q	■	59 P	60 I	61 O	■	62 Q	63 H	64 K	65 E	■	66 B
67 D	68 O	■	69 I	70 T	71 G	■	72 M	73 L	74 F	75 W	■	76 Z	77 P
78 I	79 R	■	80 K	81 U	■	82 F	83 L	84 V	■	85 A	86 N	87 R	88 I
89 G	■	90 M	91 I	92 G	■	93 B	94 F	95 I	96 Q	97 G	■	98 M	99 E
100 N	101 K	102 R	103 C	104 S	105 I	106 J	107 T	108 B	■	109 G	110 M	111 N	
112 H	113 R	114 I	■	115 N	116 Y	117 U	118 R	119 S	120 J	■	121 F	122 E	
123 I	124 A	125 Y	126 M	■	127 I	128 B	129 A	130 J	■	131 I	132 D	■	133 E
134 G	135 Z	136 I	■	137 P	138 F	139 T	140 J	141 L	■	142 Q	143 N	144 K	145 H
■	146 F	147 M	148 E	■	149 H	150 I	151 N	152 G	153 R	154 H	155 K	156 X	157 F
■	158 L	159 X	■	160 N	161 Q	162 N	163 Y	164 G	165 T	166 I	■	167 Q	168 V
■	169 F	170 T	171 R	172 X	173 D	■	174 V	175 I	176 G	■	177 N	178 T	179 Z
180 N	181 J	182 G	183 P	184 M	185 F	186 O	187 I	188 V	■	189 J	190 O	191 E	192 S
■	193 C	194 Y	195 G	■	196 I	197 G	198 Q	■	199 H	200 L	201 J	■	202 W
203 Z	204 N	■	205 M	206 V	207 Y	■	208 I	209 F	210 M	211 T	212 R	213 B	214 H	215 O

103

SINS AND
OTHER FAULTS

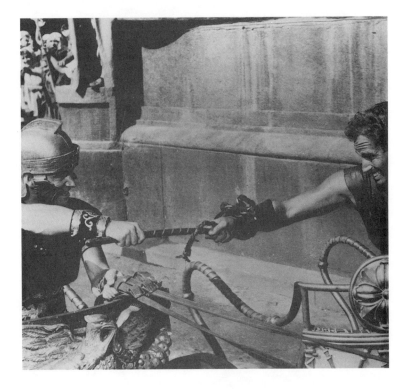

Hey, you're tailgating.

(Answers to the puzzles in Chapter 7 can be found on pages 189–191.)

185. The lords of the Philistines bribed Delilah to betray her lover, Samson, with the promise of _____.

   a. 1,100 pieces of silver from each of them

   b. the murder of Samson's wife

   c. a husband even more desirable than Samson

   d. the finest grove of lemon trees in the land

186. Lot's incestuous daughters seduced him to _____.

   a. express their dislike and disrespect

   b. do as their peers in Sodom

   c. arouse the jealousy of their mother

   d. become pregnant and carry on Lot's line

187. Why was God displeased with the people who built the Tower of Babel?

   a. They were trying to make the tower reach to Heaven.

   b. They had trafficked in the sale of icons to raise money for construction.

   c. The Tower inclined toward the wicked city of Nineveh.

   d. They were so distracted by their edifice that they were neglecting Him.

188. In his old age King David adopted the novel custom of greeting all visitors to his chambers, including his wife, Bathsheba, _____.

   a. by asking who was the wiser, himself or Solomon

   b. with the words, "Don't speak; I only want to look at you."

   c. with a young girl lying next to him for warmth

   d. with a naughty limerick

189. Adam rationalized his disobedience in eating fruit from the Tree of Knowledge by saying that _____.

   a. he had wanted to be wise enough to be conversant with God.

   b. he had given way to Eve's example.

   c. his curiosity had gotten the better of him.

   d. a serpent had told him that it was God's will.

190. Though exemplary in his conduct, Joseph learned the power of a woman's scorn when _____.

   a. his betrothed was sent into exile

   b. he was forced to lie with a diseased harlot

   c. he was made a eunuch

   d. he was arrested on the trumped-up charge of adultery

191. Moses was guilty of the crime of _____.

   a. idolatry

   b. covetousness

   c. arson

   d. murder

192. Delilah asked the superman Samson what would have to be done for him to lose his strength and to be taken prisoner. He replied that she should _____.

   a. bind him with seven green withs that were never dried

   b. bind his feet with new ropes

   c. weave the seven locks of his head

   d. undo his girdle as he slept

108

193. The first adulterer was _____.

   a. Cain

   b. Abraham

   c. Adam

   d. Lot's wife

194. Jonah spent the three days and three nights in the belly of a great fish _____.

   a. praying and crying to the Lord

   b. bemoaning the luck of the cast lots

   c. jotting down his memoirs

   d. vowing revenge on his enemies

195. During their battle with the Philistines for Canaan, the Israelites violated the law of the Lord by _____.

   a. fighting on the Sabbath

   b. neglecting to pray to Him each morning and each evening

   c. taking the Ark of the Covenant to the battlefield

   d. using children in warfare

196. While waiting for her murderers to kill her, Queen Jezebel _____.

   a. became penitent

   b. plotted to avenge her murderers

   c. arranged her hair seductively and put on makeup

   d. read the Law and the Prophets

SINNERS ANONYMOUS

We all know that the wages of sin is death, but sometimes the penalty is carried out in a creative way. Match each famous sinner with the sin and the wages thereof.

	SIN	SINNER	WAGES
___ ___	1. Tempting a woman off her diet	a. Jonah	i. Burned up in a giant fireworks display
___ ___	2. Conspired to cheat the church of money	b. Michal	ii. Tormented by frogs, locusts, death, and other unpleasantries
___ ___	3. Seduced a neighbor's wife	c. Eli	iii. Had one of the first submarine rides
___ ___	4. Kept cancelling Israel's exit visa	d. David	iv. His kingship was promised to someone else
___ ___	5. Complained about traveling conditions once too often	e. Martha	v. Fell over in his chair and broke his neck the same day his sons died
___ ___	6. Partied continually and volunteered to assault angels	f. Satan	vi. Was struck dumb
___ ___	7. Yelled at her husband for dancing naked in the streets	g. Jezebel	vii. Followed her husband to an immediate death

___ ___	8. Didn't believe an angel telling him his wife would have a baby	h. Sapphira	viii. Killed by his brother at a mutton roast
___ ___	9. Didn't discipline his priestly sons who caroused and ate temple meat	i. Saul	ix. Was made barren
___ ___	10. Seduced his half sister, a princess, and then abandoned her	j. Miriam	x. Dogs ate her blood, as prophecied
___ ___	11. Squabbled with her sister in front of dinner guests	k. Pharaoh	xi. Had to crawl on his belly for life
___ ___	12. Treated his beast of burden harshly	l. Sodom and Gomorrah	xii. Was cursed with fighting children and otherwise disruptive relatives
___ ___	13. Cancelled his revival services at the last minute	m. Balaam	xiii. Wandered 40 years in the wilderness
___ ___	14. Started a ritual sacrifice without waiting for the local prophet	n. Amnon	xiv. Was made leprous for seven days

___ ___ 15.	Discrim- inated against a prophet be- cause of his foreign wife	o. Zacharias

xv. Was publicly told to "cool out" by Jesus

___ ___ 16.	Killed a man be- cause she wanted a garden	p. Israelites

xvi. Severe chas- tisement by an angel of the Lord

197. King Ahab of Israel vexed the Lord by marrying Jezebel, daughter of a Phoenician ruler. She was displeasing to the Lord because she _____.

    a. used devices to prevent conception

    b. was cursed with sickly ambition

    c. mocked the purity of womanhood

    d. worshipped Baal

198. Often the children of great men turn out to be a disap- pointment. The sons of the prophet Samuel, a man of great faith, _____.

    a. renounced their faith

    b. turned to graft, betraying their trust as judges

    c. resorted to thievery and blackmail

    d. raised their hands against him in his frailty

199. What precipitated Cain's murder of his brother, Abel?

    a. Adam favored his younger son.

    b. God preferred the offerings of Abel.

    c. Satan tricked him into murder.

    d. Abel had committed adultery with Cain's wife.

200. In his old age, King Solomon displeased God by
_____.

   a. his vanity and arrogance
   b. his excessive love of riches and splendor
   c. worshipping gods of other nations
   d. desecrating the temple

201. Among David's children, there cannot be found a
_____.

   a. murderer
   b. rapist
   c. highway robber
   d. son who tried to overthrow him

202. Eli was the priest who reared Samuel and served the
nation of Israel. His sons _____.

   a. treated offerings with disrespect
   b. extracted tribute money from the people
   c. worshipped the gods of the Egyptians
   d. shaved half their father's beard in his sleep

203. Jacob was the father of twelve sons from whom God's
chosen people, the twelve tribes of Israel, descended.
His twelve sons were a bit wild, however, guilty of all
but which of the following?

   a. slaughtering a whole city
   b. mistreating a daughter-in-law
   c. selling their father's cattle
   d. selling their least favorite brother into slavery

204. Isaac, the only son of Abraham and Sarah, was the father of the nation Israel. But his twin sons, Jacob and Esau, didn't make life easy. They did everything *but* _____.

    a. fight over a birthright

    b. plot to murder the other brother

    c. marry foreign girls

    d. get drunk every night of the week

205. King David was entranced by the sight of Bathsheba bathing on her roof. Lust got the better of him, despite her marriage to Uriah. To have her for himself, David _____.

    a. sent several soldiers to arrest her for indecent exposure

    b. wrote her a song telling of God's will that she marry him

    c. told her of Uriah's faithlessness and promised her a home in the palace once she divorced him

    d. ordered Uriah to the front lines of battle, where he was promptly killed

206. After defeating the Amalekites, King Saul incurred the Lord's wrath for his disobedience in _____.

    a. bringing back the enemies' livestock instead of destroying them

    b. taking all the credit of the victory for himself

    c. ignoring the prophet Samuel's blessing

    d. bringing a slave girl back to his palace

207. Jacob, an ambitious young man, stole the blessing due his twin brother Esau by pulling a fast one on their father. The deception worked because he _____.

    a. got his father drunk before the blessing

    b. bribed Esau with half his inheritance

c. dressed up in his brother's clothes and some assorted goatskins to disguise his smooth skin

d. told his father that Esau had rejected the God of Abraham

208. David sinned in numbering the people. The punishment entailed _____.

a. David's being exiled for seven years

b. the death of 70,000 men

c. a seven-year drought

d. a postponement of the building of the Temple for forty years

209. Drunkenness was a weakness of _____.

a. Noah

b. King Saul

c. Lot

d. Jonah

210. What quality led Jonah to end up in the belly of a great fish?

a. procrastination

b. laziness

c. cowardice

d. pride

211. Queen Jezebel of Israel plotted the murder of Naboth because _____.

a. Naboth had spread the word that she was a harlot

b. he had seduced her and was threatening to tell her husband

c. her husband, King Ahab, coveted Naboth's vineyard

d. he had criticized her ostentatious clothing and painted face

I HAVE BUT ONE REGRET...

Identify who made the famous mistake.

"Next time...

_____ 1. I won't eat fruit off of strange trees."
_____ 2. I'll go and preach one little sermon in Nineveh."
_____ 3. I won't take one final look at the old hometown."
_____ 4. I'll take any neighbor who builds a boat seriously."
_____ 5. I won't mess with the Ark of the Covenant."
_____ 6. I won't give in to peer pressure when trying an innocent man."
_____ 7. I won't get discouraged and go home in the middle of a missionary journey."
_____ 8. I'll go without the vineyard my husband wants so much."
_____ 9. I won't taunt any little kid with a slingshot."
_____ 10. I won't ride the getaway mule under any low trees."
_____ 11. I won't take baths out in open air."
_____ 12. I won't start the war without the prophet."
_____ 13. I won't go to sleep near any woman with scissors."
_____ 14. I won't start to doubt until I'm back in the boat."
_____ 15. I won't attempt to dispose of the queen's uncle."
_____ 16. I won't get carried away by my niece's dancing."
_____ 17. I won't show favoritism toward only one son."
_____ 18. I won't steal any war booty and hide it in my tent."

116

212. Having a millstone cast around one's neck was
_____.

    a. a means of public humiliation

    b. a method to insure drowning

    c. the symbol of being unjustly burdened

    d. a penance for minor misdemeanors

213. In the last hours of His life in the Garden of Gethsemane, Jesus was disappointed with His disciples because
_____.

    a. they would not put away their wine and revelry

    b. they were sleeping instead of praying

    c. their weeping mocked His immortality

    d. they refused to believe that His hour was at hand

214. The apostle Thomas got his nickname by doubting
_____.

    a. his calling as a disciple

    b. the resurrection of Jesus

    c. that Jesus was the Messiah

    d. the promise of the Holy Spirit

215. As a reward for her exotic dancing on his birthday, the fetching Salome was offered up to half of Herod's kingdom. But she asked for _____.

    a. two thirds of his kingdom

    b. his loins in marriage

    c. a Roman officer to be her slave

    d. the head of the imprisoned John the Baptist

216. Jesus walked on the water and invited Peter to join Him. Peter _____.

    a. got cold feet

    b. sank, for lack of faith

    c. begged Jesus to get back into the boat

    d. wanted John to go ahead of him

217. Three of the gospel writers believed that Judas betrayed Jesus strictly for the thirty pieces of silver. But Luke saw _____.

    a. the evil hand of Satan

    b. an underlying jealousy

    c. an ambition to assume the leadership of Jesus

    d. the settling of an old grudge

218. While abducting Jesus, the multitude with swords and staves tried to seize "a certain young man" who had been dogging Him. The youth _____.

    a. was carrying a dagger and presumably was intent on assassination

    b. claimed that Jesus was his father

    c. shucked his clothes and ran away

    d. threatened suicide if restrained

219. In Gethsemane, no attempt was made to arrest Jesus' disciples, most of whom _____.

    a. followed the procession to the high priest Caiaphas

    b. forsook Him and ran away

    c. knelt in prayer

    d. were prostrate with grief

220. As He was being arrested, Jesus reproved His disciple Simon Peter for _____.

a. cutting off an ear of a servant of the high priest

b. holding on to the hem of His garment

c. being faithless with so much weeping

d. vowing revenge on Judas

221. Upon being accused of associating with Jesus, Peter _____.

a. angrily threw an empty vase at the girl who had accused him

b. vehemently denied that he had ever known Him

c. drew his sword and threatened to kill Jesus himself

d. leaped out an open window and went into hiding

222. Zebedee's wife, very proud of her sons James and John, asked Jesus to promote them to _____.

a. leadership in the coming church

b. experts in the working of miracles

c. a seat on either side of Jesus in the Heavenly Kingdom

d. a special place on the Mountain of the Tranfiguration

223. Even traveling evangelists had their share of spats that led to irreparable splits. Paul and Barnabas were no exception, splitting up over _____.

a. Gentiles being given the same gospel as Jews

b. expanding their ministry beyond Asia Minor

c. disciplining wayward Christians in Corinth

d. keeping John Mark on the evangelistic team

224. The sin of the church of Laodicea that made God want to spew them out of His mouth was _____.

   a. idolatry to heathen idols

   b. forcing Jewish law on Gentile converts

   c. lukewarmness in their devotion to God

   d. adultery and fornication

THE WEAKNESS OF THE FLESH: A DOUBLE ACROSTIC

The double acrostic on the next few pages, spell a verse dealing with human frailty. Fill in the answers you might already know and put the letters in the corresponding numbered squares in the grid. If you are stumped for an answer, you can work backward from the grid, using the letters you have already filled in as clues. On the grid itself, the shaded squares indicate spaces between words.

A. And the earth brought forth grass, and herb yielding seed after his kind, and the tree yielding fruit, whose seed was in itself, after his kind: and God saw that it was good. And the evening and the morning were the $\overline{62}$ $\overline{5}$ $\overline{109}$ $\overline{3}$ $\overline{124}$ $\overline{22}$ $\overline{72}$ $\overline{169}$. (Gen. 1:12–13)

B. And the Lord God called unto Adam, and said unto him, Where $\overline{68}$ $\overline{127}$ $\overline{158}$ $\overline{50}$ $\overline{81}$ $\overline{57}$ $\overline{18}$? And he said, I heard thy voice in the garden, and I was afraid, because I was naked; and I hid myself. (Gen. 3:9–10.)

C. So he drove out the man; and he placed at the east of the garden of Eden Cherubims, and a $\overline{1}$ $\overline{146}$ $\overline{119}$ $\overline{67}$ $\overline{35}$ $\overline{16?}$ $\overline{130}$ $\overline{134}$ $\overline{77}$ $\overline{9}$ $\overline{91}$ $\overline{66}$ which turned every way, to keep the way of the tree of life. (Gen. 3:24)

D. And Jacob was left alone; and there wrestled a man with him until the breaking of the day. And when he saw that he prevailed not against him, he touched the hollow of (Jacob's) $\overline{51}$ $\overline{99}$ $\overline{42}$ $\overline{187}$ $\overline{161}$. (Gen. 32:24–25)

E. Thou shalt not suffer a $\overline{210}$ $\overline{140}$ $\overline{192}$ $\overline{63}$ $\overline{12}$ to live. (Exod. 22:18)

F. And if it seem evil unto you to serve the Lord, choose you this day whom ye will serve; whether the gods which your fathers served that were on the other side of the flood, or the gods of the Amorites, in whose land ye dwell; but as for me and my house, we will $\overline{174}$ $\overline{199}$ $\overline{95}$ $\overline{34}$ $\overline{86}$ $\overline{125}$ $\overline{159}$ $\overline{112}$ $\overline{83}$ $\overline{147}$ $\overline{145}$ $\overline{20}$. (Josh. 24:15)

G. And she made him sleep upon her knees; and she called for a man, and she caused him to $\overline{203}$ $\overline{71}$ $\overline{53}$ $\overline{177}$ $\overline{100}$ off the seven locks of his head; and she began to afflict him, and his strength went from him. (Judg. 16:19)

H. And (David) wrote in the letter, saying, Set ye Uriah in the forefront of the $\overline{198}$ $\overline{79}$ $\overline{205}$ $\overline{117}$ $\overline{154}$ $\overline{213}$ $\overline{107}$ battle, and retire ye from him, that he may be smitten, and die. (II Sam. 11:15)

121

I. And David comforted __ __ __ __-sheba his wife, and went
   101 75 30 204
   in unto her, and lay with her. (II Sam. 12:24)

J. His strength shall be hungerbitten, and destruction shall be
   ready at his __ __ __ __ . It shall devour the strength of
              150 39 189 90
   his skin. (Job 18:12–13)

K. What is man, that thou art __ __ __ __ __ __ __ of him?
                              168 74 155 85 94 129 19
   (Ps. 8:4)

L. __ __ __ __ __ __ __ __ __ __ said in his heart,
   4 52 65 173 211 44 201 196 113 152 118
   There is no God. (Ps. 14:1)

M. By thee have I been holden up from the womb: thou art
   he __ __ __ __ __ __ __ __ __ __ __ __ __ of my
      98 115 82 11 195 105 151 121 92 178 123 28 73
   mother bowels: my praise shall be continually of thee. (Ps.
   71:6)

N. Trust in the Lord with all thine heart; and lean not unto
   thine own understanding. In all thy ways acknowledge him,
   and he __ __ __ __ __ __ __ __ __ __ __ thy paths.
          80 138 209 87 46 10 157 148 61 40 114
   (Prov. 3:5–6).

O. Is there no __ __ __ __ in Gilead; is there no physician
                190 183 36 76
   there? (Jer. 8:22)

P. They shall beat their __ __ __ __ __ __ into plowshares.
                         136 193 58 139 166 110
   (Mic. 4:3)

Q. Take therefore no thought for the morrow: for the morrow
   shall take thought for the things of itself. Sufficient unto

the day is $\overline{}_{29}$ $\overline{}_{126}$ $\overline{}_{133}$ $\overline{}_{33}$ $\overline{}_{89}$ $\overline{}_{164}$ $\overline{}_{84}$ $\overline{}_{160}$ $\overline{}_{180}$ $\overline{}_{93}$ $\overline{}_{60}$ $\overline{}_{171}$ $\overline{}_{143}$ $\overline{}_{200}$. (Matt. 6:34)

R. Watch therefore: for ye know not what hour your Lord
$\overline{}_{111}$ $\overline{}_{49}$ $\overline{}_{54}$ $\overline{}_{64}$ $\overline{}_{137}$ $\overline{}_{17}$ $\overline{}_{97}$ $\overline{}_{181}$. (Matt. 24:42)

S. And if thy $\overline{}_{106}$ $\overline{}_{188}$ $\overline{}_{23}$ $\overline{}_{179}$ $\overline{}_{25}$ $\overline{}_{186}$ $\overline{}_{212}$ $\overline{}_{207}$ $\overline{}_{69}$ $\overline{}_{149}$ thee, cut it off. (Mark 9:45)

T. If any man will come after me, let him deny himself, and take up his cross $\overline{}_{47}$ $\overline{}_{13}$ $\overline{}_{88}$ $\overline{}_{182}$ $\overline{}_{104}$, and follow me. (Luke 9:23)

U. For the labourer is worthy of $\overline{}_{206}$ $\overline{}_{21}$ $\overline{}_{141}$ $\overline{}_{38}$ $\overline{}_{194}$ $\overline{}_{176}$ $\overline{}_{6}$.(Luke 10:7)

V. And he saith unto him, Out of thine $\overline{}_{128}$ $\overline{}_{43}$ $\overline{}_{215}$ $\overline{}_{163}$ $\overline{}_{2}$ $\overline{}_{191}$ $\overline{}_{26}$ $\overline{}_{78}$ will I judge thee, thou wicked servant. Thou knewest that I was an austere man, taking up that I laid not down, and reaping that I did not sow. (Luke 19:22)

W. But glory, honour, and peace, to every man that worketh good, to the $\overline{}_{132}$ $\overline{}_{175}$ $\overline{}_{37}$ first, and also to the $\overline{}_{7}$ $\overline{}_{32}$ $\overline{}_{24}$ $\overline{}_{197}$ $\overline{}_{167}$ $\overline{}_{172}$ $\overline{}_{202}$. (Rom. 2:10)

X. $\overline{}_{14}$ $\overline{}_{31}$ $\overline{}_{102}$ $\overline{}_{144}$ $\overline{}_{122}$ $\overline{}_{153}$ I speak with the tongues of men and of angels. (I Cor. 13:1)

Y. For I suppose I was not a $\overline{}_{184}$ $\overline{}_{108}$ $\overline{}_{15}$ $\overline{}_{70}$ behind the very chiefest spostles. (II Cor. 11:5)

Z. There is neither Jew nor Greek, there is neither $\underset{27}{\rule{1em}{0.4pt}}$ $\underset{185}{\rule{1em}{0.4pt}}$ $\underset{120}{\rule{1em}{0.4pt}}$ $\underset{103}{\rule{1em}{0.4pt}}$ nor free, there is neither male nor female: for ye are all one in Christ Jesus. (Gal. 3:28)

AA. Drink no longer water, but use a little $\underset{156}{\rule{1em}{0.4pt}}$ $\underset{116}{\rule{1em}{0.4pt}}$ $\underset{48}{\rule{1em}{0.4pt}}$ $\underset{162}{\rule{1em}{0.4pt}}$ for thy stomach's sake and thine often infirmities. (I Tim. 5:23)

BB. Beloved, $\underset{214}{\rule{1em}{0.4pt}}$ $\underset{16}{\rule{1em}{0.4pt}}$ $\underset{55}{\rule{1em}{0.4pt}}$ $\underset{170}{\rule{1em}{0.4pt}}$ $\underset{41}{\rule{1em}{0.4pt}}$ above all things that thou mayest prosper and be in health, even as thy soul prospereth. (III John 2)

CC. I know thy works, that thou are neither hot nor cold; I $\underset{59}{\rule{1em}{0.4pt}}$ $\underset{96}{\rule{1em}{0.4pt}}$ $\underset{135}{\rule{1em}{0.4pt}}$ $\underset{208}{\rule{1em}{0.4pt}}$ $\underset{56}{\rule{1em}{0.4pt}}$ $\underset{142}{\rule{1em}{0.4pt}}$ $\underset{131}{\rule{1em}{0.4pt}}$ $\underset{8}{\rule{1em}{0.4pt}}$ $\underset{45}{\rule{1em}{0.4pt}}$ wert cold or hot. So then because thou art lukewarm and neither cold nor hot, I will spue thee out of my mouth. (Rev. 3:15-16)

	C 1	V 2	A 3		L 4	A 5	U 6		W 7	CC 8	C 9	N 10	
M 11	E 12	T 13	X 14		Y 15		BB 16	R 17	B 18	K 19	F 20		U 21
	A 22	S 23		W 24	S 25	V 26		Z 27	M 28	Q 29		I 30	X 31
W 32		Q 33	F 34	C 35	O 36		W 37	U 38	J 39	N 40	BB 41		D 42
	V 43	L 44	CC 45	N 46	T 47		AA 48	R 49	B 50		D 51	L 52	G 53
R 54		BB 55		CC 56	B 57		P 58		CC 59	Q 60	N 61	A 62	E 63
R 64	L 65	C 66		C 67	B 68	S 69		Y 70	G 71	A 72	M 73		K 74
	I 75	O 76		C 77	V 78	H 79		N 80	B 81	M 82	F 83	Q 84	
K 85	F 86	N 87	T 88	Q 89	J 90	C 91		M 92	Q 93		K 94	F 95	CC 96
R 97		M 98	D 99	G 100		I 101	X 102	Z 103	T 104		M 105	S 106	
H 107	Y 108	A 109	P 110		R 111	F 112	L 113	N 114	M 115		AA 116		H 117
L 118	C 119	Z 120	M 121		X 122	M 123	A 124		F 125	Q 126	B 127	V 128	K 129
C 130	CC 131		W 132	Q 133	C 134	CC 135	P 136		R 137	N 138	P 139	E 140	U 141
CC 142		Q 143	X 144	F 145		C 146	F 147	N 148	S 149		J 150	M 151	
L 152	X 153	H 154	K 155		AA 156	N 157	B 158	F 159		Q 160	D 161	AA 162	
V 163	Q 164	C 165	P 166		W 167		K 168	A 169	BB 170	Q 171	W 172	L 173	
F 174	W 175	U 176	G 177	M 178		S 179	Q 180	R 181		T 182	O 183	Y 184	
Z 185	S 186		D 187	S 188	J 189		O 190	V 191	E 192		P 193	U 194	M 195
L 196		W 197	H 198	F 199		Q 200	L 201	W 202	G 203	I 204		H 205	U 206
S 207		CC 208	N 209	E 210		L 211	S 212		H 213	BB 214	V 215		

PLACES THAT TIME PASSED BY

Who were the people worshiping the bronze idol?

(Answers to the puzzles in Chapter 8 can be found on page 192.)

225. After the flood waters receded, Noah's ark came to rest on the mountains of _____.

   a. Lebanon

   b. Ararat

   c. Greece

   d. the Sinai

226. Zionism takes its name from _____.

   a. a fertile plain in Canaan

   b. the Red Sea village to which the Hebrews were delivered from Egypt

   c. the followers of the prophet Zion

   d. a sacred hill in Jerusalem

227. The prophet Isaiah criticized the women of _____ for being "haughty" and having "wanton eyes" and "tinkling ornaments about their feet" and "changeable suits of apparel."

   a. Nazareth

   b. Jerusalem

   c. Babylon

   d. Nineveh

228. Unlike other judges, or leaders, Deborah counseled from _____.

   a. a synagogue

   b. under a palm tree

   c. an oasis in the desert

   d. a bathhouse

229. Jacob wrestled all night with an angel, earning himself a new name, Israel. In honor of the event he named the place _____.

a. Peniel

b. Bethel

c. Goshen

d. Emmanuel

230. Solomon, who had many admirers, played host to a queen who lavished on him many presents. Where was she from?

a. Alexandria

b. Lebanon

c. Sheba

d. Babylon

231. Goliath swaggered out of the camp of the _____ army to challenge Israel.

a. Babylonian

b. Philistine

c. Assyrian

d. Midianite

232. Ruth followed her mother-in-law, Naomi, back to Bethlehem, where she would eventually marry Boaz and become an ancestor of Jesus. What was her native land?

a. Edom

b. Ammon

c. Moab

d. Syria

233. Though He often returned to _____ during His ministry, Jesus was to pronounce its sinfulness worse than that of Sodom.

   a. Bethany

   b. Hebron

   c. Jericho

   d. Capernaum

234. The birth and the death of Jesus are highlighted with such place names as Bethlehem, Jerusalem, Bethany, Gethsemane, and Calvary, all of which are within _____ miles of one another.

   a. 5

   b. 25

   c. 35

   d. 65

235. John the Baptist conducted most of his baptisms in the _____.

   a. Sea of Galilee

   b. Mediterranean

   c. River Jordan

   d. Dead Sea

SUCH MEMORABLE PLACES

In the grid are 26 Biblical places which you must first identify from the clues and verses listed below. The initial letter of each place-name has also been given. After writing them in the blanks below, then find them in the grid on the next page.

CLUE		VERSE
1. Where Jacob had his dream about the ladder	B_____	Gen. 28:19
2. The birthplace of Jesus	B_____	Luke 2:4
3. The city where the temple was located	J_____	Mark: 11:11
4. & 5.The two nations Satan deceives and gathers together for battle	G_____ M_____	Rev. 20:8
6. One of the two cities destroyed by brimstone and fire.	S_____	Gen. 19:24
7. The river that was turned to blood	N_____	Exod. 7:20–21
8. The Promised Land	C_____	Exod. 6:4
9. Abram's birthplace	U_____	Gen. 11:27–29
10. Where Daniel's den was located	B_____	Dan. 1:1–6
11. Rahab the harlot and her household were the only survivors from this city	J_____	Josh. 6:17
12. Where Moses was given the law	S_____	Exod. 19:20
13. Noah's dock	A_____	Gen. 8:4
14. Adam and Eve's garden	E_____	Gen. 2:8
15. Where Jesus was crucified	G_____	Mark 15:22–24
16. Where the good thief crucified with Christ met him after death	P_____	Luke 23:43
17. Against the church, Jesus said, the gates of this place shall not prevail	H_____	Matt. 16:18
18. Saul's hometown	T_____	Acts 9:11
19. Jesus' hometown	N_____	Mark 1:9
20. Where Jesus met the fishermen	G_____	Matt. 4:18–19

21. On the road to this city, Saul was converted   D_____   Acts 9:3

22. Paul preached in this city, making known the "unknown god"   A_____   Acts 17:22–23

23. John had a vision on this island   P_____   Rev. 1:9

24. Joseph's caravan went to this place   E_____   Gen. 37:23–28

25. A city of Lebanon mentioned by Jesus in the same breath with Sidon   T_____   Matt. 11:22

26. Paul and Barnabas were sent on their missionary journey from this city.   A_____   Acts 13:1–3

A	R	B	E	T	H	L	E	H	E	M	E	G	A	P
Z	R	M	L	G	E	A	R	E	H	A	O	R	S	E
U	M	A	A	H	T	O	G	L	O	G	N	A	Y	N
S	O	L	R	G	E	G	A	L	E	O	A	H	O	T
H	P	O	M	A	Y	S	Y	H	M	G	G	L	A	R
T	Y	L	B	E	T	P	I	A	E	A	Y	R	O	M
N	I	L	E	D	E	N	S	D	L	B	S	P	H	E
J	S	N	E	H	T	A	E	I	A	U	I	E	T	H
T	O	O	N	U	T	H	L	B	S	R	N	U	E	S
A	M	I	D	R	C	E	T	I	U	Z	A	N	R	C
H	T	E	M	O	E	U	B	O	R	U	I	P	A	T
D	A	C	I	D	M	L	I	L	E	M	A	N	Z	A
D	P	T	O	H	C	I	R	E	J	E	A	I	A	N
P	N	H	R	S	U	C	S	A	M	A	D	A	N	I
A	M	A	Z	A	O	R	R	D	N	J	A	P	E	P

236. Golgotha, a name that has come to symbolize horror, was the _____.

   a. place in the Garden of Gethsemane where Judas betrayed Jesus

   b. site of the crucifixion of Jesus

   c. home of Satan

   d. fortified plateau where Hebrews committed mass suicide

237. Zacchaeus was known to have climbed down from a sycamore tree in answer to Jesus' invitation. What town was he from?

   a. Capernaum

   b. Jerusalem

   c. Beersheba

   d. Jericho

238. The apostles Paul and Barnabas were sent out on a missionary journey from the church in _____.

   a. Antioch

   b. Tarsus

   c. Jerusalem

   d. Damascus

239. Two disciples, distraught by the death of Jesus, were joined in their somber walk by a stranger who turned out to be their risen Lord. Where were they going?

   a. Emmaus

   b. Jerusalem

   c. Cana

   d. Bethany

240. One night, Paul had a vision of a young man imploring him to come to _____.

   a. Asia Minor

   b. Macedonia

   c. Rome

   d. Galatia

MIRACLES AND THE SUPERNATURAL

Who made Jesus carry the cross?

(Answers to the puzzles in Chapter 9 can be found on pages 193–194.)

241. Shadrach, Meshach, and Abednego were three Hebrew men in Babylon whose names have found their way into a popular song. They survived _____.

   a. submersion in the Euphrates

   b. hanging on the gallows

   c. a den of vipers

   d. a fiery furnace

242. When 100-year-old Abraham and 92-year-old Sarah learned that she was pregnant, they _____.

   a. were mortified

   b. laughed

   c. were profuse in their prayers of thanksgiving

   d. toasted the news with wine from the tenderest vines

243. Pre-empting Freud by thousands of years, _____was the first interpreter of dreams.

   a. Joseph

   b. Daniel

   c. Ezekiel

   d. Mordecai

244. The blinded Samson, his hair having grown back, regained his strength and _____.

   a. single-handedly confronted the Philistines on the battlefield

   b. threw a spear 26 miles

   c. strangled Delilah

   d. tore down the Philistine temple of Dagon, killing 3,000 people, including himself

245. During a drought visited upon Israel as a result of King Ahab's and Queen Jezebel's evil rule, God's prophet Elijah was sustained by _____.

a. the morning dew and honey

b. bread and flesh brought to him by ravens

c. eels floating in the brook Cherith

d. manna

246. In pursuit of Moses and the children of Israel, Pharaoh's cavalry drowned and "sank into the bottom as a stone" in the _____.

a. River Jordan

b. Sea of Reeds, or Red Sea

c. Tigris

d. Mediterranean

247. What is the origin of Passover?

a. God, in smiting the first-born of all families in Egypt, passed over the marked homes of the Israelites.

b. Replenishing rains passed over the land of Canaan.

c. The children of Israel passed over the River Jordan into the promised land.

d. God passed over the Jews in the desert in the form of a dove.

248. The children of Israel were guided out of Egyptian bondage by God, who took the form of _____.

a. low-flying ravens

b. a burning bush

c. pillars of cloud and fire

d. a trail of boulders

249. At the end of his ministry, Elijah passed his mantle to Elisha and _____.

   a. was taken by a chariot of fire in a whirlwind

   b. climbed Mount Horeb and was seen no more

   c. was caught up in an earthquake and disappeared

   d. vanished in a blinding light

250. *Raiders of the Lost Ark* is not the first recording of the Ark of the Covenant causing dire consequences when falling into the wrong hands. Three of the four events listed below are recorded in I Samuel. Which is not among them?

   a. Knocking the Philistine god Dagon off his pedestal in the temple.

   b. Afflicting the people of Ashdod with tumors.

   c. Striking the firstborn of the Amalekites with blindness.

   d. Killing 50,070 men of Bethshemesh because they dared to look inside.

251. When Pharaoh would not allow the children of Israel to leave Egypt, a number of plagues struck the land. Which of these was not one of them?

   a. gnats

   b. scorpions

   c. frogs

   d. locusts

252. Which of the following was not one of Elijah's miracles?

   a. calling fire down from Heaven

   b. parting the waters of the River Jordan

   c. multiplying food

   d. purifying water

141

253. Angels ministered to Jesus twice during His ministry. The first time was _____.

   a. when He talked with the elders in the temple

   b. after He had fasted in the wilderness

   c. before He chose the twelve apostles

   d. just after He was baptized by John

254. When an angel appeared to Samson's parents to announce his birth, they asked him his name. He replied, _____.

   a. Michael

   b. Gabriel

   c. It is known only to God

   d. It is a secret name of wonder

WHAT TO SAY TO A BURNING BUSH

(AND OTHER HELPFUL SUGGESTIONS)

Below is a list of men and women who actually saw and spoke to God. Match the people with what they saw and their response to their heavenly visitation.

PERSON	GOD'S MANIFES-TATION	PERSON'S REACTION
__ __ 1. Jacob	a. three men	i. to hide
__ __ 2. Moses	b. looked like a gardener	ii. to make a huge picnic under a tree
__ __ 3. Isaiah	c. the Lord stood above a ladder into the heavens	iii. run to tell the disciples

142

___ ___	4. Ezekiel	d. a still, small voice after an earthquake, wind, and fire	iv. to make a marker out of a pillow
___ ___	5. Stephen	e. one like the Son of God in the fire	v. to eat a scroll, as suggested
___ ___	6. Abraham	f. talked through a burning bush	vi. to decree that anyone who spoke against Shadrach, Meshach, and Abednego's God would be cut into pieces
___ ___	7. Adam and Eve	g. he was high and lifted up, and his train filled the temple	vii. to complain that he was the only faithful servant left in the world
___ ___	8. Elijah	h. Jesus sat on the right hand of God	viii. to cry, "Woe is me!" and an angel came and put a coal on his lips
___ ___	9. Mary Magdalene	i. his voice walked through the garden	ix. to be cast out of the city and stoned to death
___ ___	10. Nebuchadnezzar	j. he was on a throne, half amber and half fire, surrounded by a rainbow	x. to take off his shoes

143

DREAMS & VISIONS

People frequently heard messages from God through dreams and visions. Match the people with the dreams and visions they had.

_____ 1. A man Paul knew a. had a vision of dry bones taking on flesh and life

_____ 2. Nebuchadnezzar b. dreamed of a ladder stretching to heaven

_____ 3. Pharaoh c. was told in a vision to pray for Saul of Tarsus

_____ 4. Samuel d. was promised in a vision that he would have a son

_____ 5. wise men e. was caught up into the third heaven

_____ 6. Jacob f. had a vision of a magnificent throne surrounded by 24 elders

_____ 7. Ananias g. was told by an angel to send men to Joppa for Peter

_____ 8. Solomon h. saw the Lord on a throne with the seraphim above him

_____ 9. Joseph i. was shown animals let down in a sheet

_____ 10. Cornelius j. saw Gabriel explained the meaning of the 70 weeks in a vision

_____ 11. Ezekiel k. was offered anything he wanted by God

_____ 12. Zacharias l. dreamed of a great image broken into many pieces

_____ 13. Abraham m. saw the glory of God, and Jesus standing at His right hand

_____ 14. John

_____ 15. Stephen

_____ 16. Daniel

_____ 17. Peter

_____ 18. Isaiah

n. was told in a dream of his son's birth and was stricken dumb

o. received a warning from God not to return to Herod

p. dreamed of fat and lean cattle symbolizing famine on the heels of plenty

q. received a warning from God of the judgment that was to come to Eli's house

r. dreamed that his family would bow down to him

255. Angels take on different appearances when talking to men. In which of the following guises did an angel *not* appear?

a. as a great eagle, with great wings

b. as a flaming stone

c. with a face like lightning

d. as a wheel in the midst of a wheel

256. Satan was also an angel. In the Bible, he does *not* appear as _____.

a. a serpent

b. a tempter in the wilderness

c. an evil spirit that entered people

d. a figure in fiery red

257. There is a tendency to associate miracles with Jesus. But a great many occurred in the Old Testament. Which of these is unique to the New Testament?

a. Many men are fed with few loaves.

b. A deadly pottage is cured with meal.

c. The waters of Jericho are healed with salt.

d. Angels open a prison.

258. High on a mountain, the disciples Peter, James, and John saw Jesus talking with _____.

a. Moses and Elijah (Elias)

b. birds and bees

c. a burning bush

d. the high priest Melchizedek

259. Which one of Jesus' miracles is recorded by all the evangelists?

a. His walking on the sea

b. His making wine from water at Cana

c. His feeding 5,000 people on five loaves and two fishes

d. His raising Lazarus from the dead

260. After Jesus was baptized by his cousin, John the Baptist, _____.

a. He asked John to become one of His disciples

b. He asked to be left alone to meditate

c. He cleansed the lepers of their fleshly woes

d. the Spirit of God descended upon Him in the form of a dove

261. Upon driving the demons out of a deranged man and into a herd of 2,000 pigs, Jesus was set upon by the people of Gadarenes, who _____.

    a. embraced Him as their new god

    b. were enraged and demanded compensation for their swine

    c. were afraid and prayed that He would go away

    d. engaged mercenaries to slay Him

262. Jesus fed the multitude of 5,000. His "starter provisions" consisted of _____.

    a. four sacks of wheat and a flagon of honey

    b. five barley loaves and two fishes

    c. unleavened bread and a pitcher of wine

    d. a bundle of chaff and an ewe

263. Jesus' miracle of restoring sight to a blind man involved _____.

    a. spitting

    b. cursing

    c. praying

    d. blindfolding

264. After raising the twelve-year-old daughter of Jairus from the dead, Jesus said, "_____"

    a. Don't tell anyone.

    b. All who believe can be resurrected.

    c. It was unjust that a good child should die so young.

    d. Is not this proof that I am the Son of God?

265. What phenomenon occurred during the crucifixion?

   a. Three rainbows filled the sky.

   b. Darkness fell over the land.

   c. Crosses appeared on the foreheads of the multitude.

   d. The sun stood still.

266. On learning of the miracles of Jesus, King Herod said,
   "_____"

   a. They must be the work of John the Baptist, risen from the dead.

   b. Bring the impostor to me immediately.

   c. Put no credence in heresy.

   d. The Roman powers would be none too pleased with such a troublemaker.

267. Paul and Silas were jailed in Philippi for curing a sorceress of her prophetic powers, thus depriving her "masters" of income. The pair converted their jailkeeper to Christianity by _____.

   a. their cheerfulness and prayers to Jesus

   b. staying in the prison after an earthquake had destroyed the walls

   c. promising that if he believed, a miracle would happen to him

   d. the rapid healing of the bodily wounds that the magistrate had inflicted upon them

268. On being received into Heaven, Jesus _____.

   a. began to carve the Sermon on the Mount on tablets

   b. kissed his Father and said, "It is finished"

   c. asked to speak one last time to His disciples

   d. sat on the right hand of God

269. The arrival of Pentecost was marked by

    a. a dove descending upon the temple

    b. a multitude of heavenly hosts praising God

    c. a plague of locusts

    d. tongues of fire and a babble of languages

270. In explaining the significance of Pentecost to the amazed multitudes, Peter cited a prophecy of Joel that included all but which one of the following?

    a. Your sons and daughters will prophesy.

    b. Your young men will see visions.

    c. Your children will teach the wise.

    d. Your old men will dream dreams.

271. When Jesus fed the 5,000, he began with five loaves and two fish. After everyone had had his fill, how much was left over?

    a. nothing

    b. five basketsful

    c. five loaves and two fish

    d. twelve basketsful

272. What miracle caused the woman at the well to believe that Jesus was no ordinary Jew seeking to quench his thirst, but a prophet?

    a. He revealed her checkered past to her.

    b. He caused water to gush from the well.

    c. He forgave her sins of adultery.

    d. He answered her everything she asked about the Law and the Prophets.

COMPLETE YOUR FAVORITE BIBLE PASSAGE

The boy who was a stone's throw away from victory.

(Answers to the puzzles in Chapter 10 can be found on pages 195–198.)

FINISH THE PROVERB

Finish the proverb.

_____ 1. A soft answer

_____ 2. A word fitly spoken

_____ 3. A merry heart

_____ 4. A good name

_____ 5. The fear of the Lord

_____ 6. He that keepeth the law,

_____ 7. Open rebuke

_____ 8. Whoso boasteth himself of a false gift

_____ 9. A fool

_____ 10. He that trusteth in his own heart

_____ 11. A woman that feareth the Lord

_____ 12. The path of the just

_____ 13. The fruit of the righteous

_____ 14. A virtuous woman

_____ 15. Hope deferred

a. is like clouds and wind without rain.

b. uttereth all his mind.

c. maketh the heart sick.

d. is a fool.

e. is a tree of life.

f. is as the shining light.

g. turneth away wrath.

h. is rather to be chosen than great riches.

i. . . . shall be praised.

j. maketh a cheerful countenance.

k. is like apples of gold in pictures of silver.

l. is a crown to her husband.

m. is better than secret love.

n. happy is he.

o. is the beginning of knowledge.

PSALM 23

Test your memory of this favorite psalm by filling in the blanks and then using the words to complete the criss-cross puzzle.

The _____ is my _____; I shall not _____. He _____ me to _____ down in green _____: he _____ me beside the still _____. He _____ my _____: he leadeth _____ in the _____ of _____ for his name's _____. Yea, though I _____ through the _____ of the _____ of _____, I will _____ no _____: for _____ art with me; thy _____ and thy _____, they _____ me. Thou preparest a _____ before me in the _____ of mine _____: thou _____ my _____ with _____; my _____ runneth over. Surely _____ and _____ shall _____ me all the _____ of my _____: and I will _____ in the _____ of the Lord for ever.

IN PRAISE OF LOVE (CHARITY)

I Corinthians 13 was written by the apostle Paul as an answer to the spiritual one-upmanship that was dividing the church. Though such controversy still continues, this chapter on love remains one of the most quoted passages of the Bible. Complete verses 1 and 2 by filling in the appropriate words in the column on the right. Then unscramble the circled letters to determine the context in which Paul so eloquently urges us all to love. (If you need a clue, see chapter 14, verse 1.)

Though I speak with the _____ of men and of _____, and have not _____, I am become as sounding _____, or a _____ cymbal. And though I have the gift of _____, and understand all _____, and all _____; and though I have all _____, so that I could remove _____, and have not charity, I am _____.

a. _ _ _ _ ◯ _ ◯
b. ◯ _ _ _ _ _
c. _ _ _ _ ◯ _ _
d. _ ◯ _ _ _
e. _ _ _ _ _ ◯ _ _
f. ◯ _ _ _ _ _ _
g. _ _ _ ◯ _ _ _ _ ◯
h. _ _ _ _ _ ◯ _ _ ◯ _
i. ◯ _ _ _ _
j. _ _ _ _ _ _ ◯ _ _
k. _ _ ◯ _ _ _ _

_ _ _ _ _ _ _ _ _   _ _ _ _ _

273. The book of Proverbs declares that many friends are made by _____.

a. wealth

b. a winning smile

c. listening and soft words

d. a stout heart and a firm hand

156

274. "A merry heart _____."

    a. maketh a cheerful countenance

    b. hath a continual feast

    c. doeth good like a medicine

    d. doth bless a man and all his house

275. "Happy is the man that hath his quiver full of them—that is, full of _____."

    a. dreams

    b. children

    c. songs

    d. friends

276. In the sensuous Song of Solomon, the taste of fine wine is likened to _____.

    a. the silks of Cathay against bare skin

    b. the scented breeze of a summer afternoon

    c. the roof of a lover's mouth

    d. thighs bathing in warm goats milk

277. A cynical proverb has a "young man void of understanding" go to _____ as inevitably as "an ox goes to the slaughter."

    a. the winery and the granary

    b. the money-changers

    c. his couch of sloth

    d. a harlot

TEST YOUR KNOWLEDGE OF PAULINE THEOLOGY

Complete the verses from Paul's letter to the Romans. Then match the references to each verse. (Number 15 is a theologian's special.)

_____ 1. For the _____ of sin is _____;
but the _____ of God is _____
_____.

_____ 2. Therefore being justified by _____, we
have _____ with God.

_____ 3. All things _____ together for _____
to them that _____ God.

_____ 4. Whosoever shall _____ upon the ____
of the Lord shall be _____.

_____ 5. For the _____ that I would I _____
_____.

_____ 6. There is no _____ of persons with
_____.

_____ 7. Make not _____ for the _____,
to fulfil the _____ thereof.

_____ 8. Let every _____ be _____
unto the higher _____.

_____ 9. The _____ shall live by _____.

_____ 10. For we are saved by _____.

_____ 11. So we, being _____, are one _____
in Christ.

_____ 12. Present your _____ a living _____,
holy, _____ unto _____.

_____ 13. There is therefore now no _____ to them
which are in _____.

_____ 14. We are _____ with him by _____
into death.

_____ 15. I am persuaded, that neither _____, nor
_____, nor _____, nor
_____, nor _____, nor
_____ present, nor _____
to come, nor _____, nor _____,
nor any other _____ shall be able to
_____ us from the _____ of
God.

a. 1:17	f. 7:19	k. 10:13
b. 2:11	g. 8:1	l. 12:1
c. 5:1	h. 8:24	m. 12:5
d. 6:4	i. 8:28	n. 13:1
e. 6:23	j. 8:38–39	o. 13:14

278. "Faith is the substance of things hoped for, the evidence
of things _____."

a. untouchable

b. not seen

c. beyond dreams

d. to come

279. "God loveth a _____."

a. cheerful giver

b. forgiving heart

c. steadfast believer

d. repentant sinner

159

280. "The flowers appear on the earth; the time of the singing of birds is come, and the voice of the turtle is heard in our land." A verse from _____.

  a. Psalm 127

  b. the Song of Solomon

  c. Revelation

  d. Ecclesiastes

281. "Seek ye first the kingdom of God, and His righteous-ness; _____."

  a. and ye shall find that kingdom

  b. and all these things shall be added unto you

  c. and ye shall discover the Lord in all His glory

  d. and the things of the world shall fade from view

282. Jesus told His disciples that the greatest love a person can show is _____.

  a. turning away angry words with a soft answer

  b. giving himself to the keeping of God's command-ments

  c. giving half of his worldly goods to the poor

  d. the willingness to give up one's life for one's friends

283. "The Word was made _____, and dwelt among us."

  a. holy

  b. law

  c. flesh

  d. light

284. "O death, where is thy sting? O grave, where is thy
_____?"

   a. victory

   b. mercy

   c. glory

   d. exaltation

A SCRIPTURE-VERSE
CROSSWORD PUZZLE

Complete the crossword puzzle with the words used to fill in
the verses listed on these pages.

ACROSS

   1. surely goodness and _____shall follow me (Ps. 23:6)
   6. let the sea _____, and the fullness thereof (Ps. 96:11)
  11. sir, come down _____my child die (John 4:49)
  12. there is none _____name under heaven (Acts 4:12)
  14. he that trusteth in his _____shall fall (Prov. 11:28)
  16. _____ me O God and know my heart (Ps. 139:23)
  17. he gave his _____begotten son (John 3:16)
  18. the _____, which they saw in the east, went before
      them (Matt. 2:9)
  19. ...shepherds, abiding in the field, _____watch over
      their flock (Luke 2:8)
  22. do good to them that _____you (Matt. 5:44)
  24. if thy _____offend thee, cut it off (Mark 9:45)
  25. the word of the Lord endureth for _____(I Pet. 1:25)

26. let your light _____shine before men (Matt. 5:16)
28. he took the _____loaves and the fishes (Matt. 15:36)
29. and the truth shall make you _____(John 8:32)
32. _____ and Onan died in the land of Canaan (Gen. 46:12)
34. but the _____of all things is at hand (I Pet. 4:7)
35. be ye _____, unmovable, always abounding in the work . . . (I Cor. 15:58)
37. with the mouth confession is made unto _____(Rom 10:10)
39. _____ shall save his people from their sins (Matt. 1:21)
41. _____ shall judge his people (Gen. 49:16)
42. they _____not, neither do they reap (Matt. 6:26)
44. let him _____evil, and do good (I Pet. 3:11)
46. by _____man's offense death reigned (Rom. 5:17)
47. the sun knoweth his _____down (Ps. 104:19)
48. _____ thanks be to God (I Cor. 15:57)
49. _____ angel from heaven (Gal. 1:8)
50. took branches of _____trees (John 12:13)
51. lay up his words, in thine _____(Job 22:22)
52. have mercy on _____O Lord (Matt. 15:22)
53. _____ is wisdom (Rev. 13:18)
55. _____ up the gift of God which is in thee (II Tim. 1:6)
57. come now, and let us _____together (Isa. 1:18)
59. and his allowance . . . a daily _____for every day (II Kings 25:30)
61. every one of you hath a _____(I Cor. 14:26)
62. and bring to pass his _____(Isa. 28:21)
63. for as in Adam all _____, . . . (I. Cor. 15:22)
64. for these words are _____and faithful (Rev. 21:5)
65. they repented _____the preaching of Jesus (Luke 11:32)
66. for the wages of sin is _____(Rom. 3:23)
68. for as concerning this _____, we know . . . (Acts 28:22)
70. the _____is not above his master (Matt. 10:24)
72. I see men as _____walking (Mark 8:24)
74. they make a noise like a _____(Ps. 59:6)
75. I will _____before you into Galilee (Matt. 26:32)
77. add to your faith _____(II Pet. 1:5)
78. though I be free from all men, yet I made myself _____ unto all (I. Cor. 9:19)

162

79. blessed are the _____in heart (Matt. 5:8)
80. who is _____to stand before the holy God? (I Sam. 6:20)
81. the Lord shall _____from heaven (I Thess. 4:16)
82. give _____this day our daily bread (Matt. 6:11)
83. even so must the _____of man be lifted up (John 3:14)
84. as an eagle stirreth up her _____(Deut. 32:11)

DOWN

1. a good _____showeth favor (Ps. 112:5)
2. _____ unto me the joy of thy salvation (Ps. 51:12)
3. male and female _____he them (Gen. 1:27)
4. even the _____of their visitation (Jer. 11:23)
5. the Lord is my _____(Ps. 18:2)
6. and she sat beside the _____(Ruth 2:14)
7. _____ sit here under my footstool (James 2:3)
8. they made two _____of gold (Exod. 39:19)
9. whereby we _____, Abba, Father (Rom 8:15)
10. who shall _____into heaven? (Rom. 10:6)
13. let not mercy and truth forsake _____(Prov. 3:3)
15. that the _____were opened (Ezek. 1:1)
17. and many believed _____him (John 10:42)
18. thou makest it _____with showers (Ps. 65:10)
20. the serpent beguiled _____(II Cor. 11:3)
21. and Huppim, the children of _____(I Chron. 7:12)
22. and _____was sad at the saying (Mark 10:22)
23. were there not _____cleansed? (Luke 17:17)
27. the Lord blessed _____(II Sam. 6:11)
28. the _____of death is sin (I. Cor. 15:56)
30. Christ should be made of none _____(I Cor. 1:17)
31. the centurion found a ship...and he put _____therein (Acts 27:6)
33. and the _____brake in upon them (Ps. 106:29)
35. Jesus that great _____(Heb. 13:20)
36. why callest _____me good? (Matt. 19:17)
38. in the house of one Simon a _____(Acts 10:32)
40. _____ ye in at the strait gate (Matt. 7:13)

43. a foolish _____is clamorous (Prov. 9:13)
45. they behold your _____conversation... (I Peter 3:2)
48. I am the daughter of _____, the son of Milcah (Gen. 24:24)
50. he will speak _____unto his people (Ps. 85:8)
52. when the _____of the house cometh (Mark 13:35)
54. give attendance to _____(I Tim. 4:13)
56. thou shalt make a _____of pure gold (Exod. 28:36)
58. who shall _____in his holy place? (Ps. 24:3)
60. arise, go up to _____(Josh. 8:1)
61. he maketh me to lie down in green _____(Ps. 23:2)
64. shew me the _____money. And they brought unto him a penny. (Matt. 22:19)
67. glory to God in the _____(Luke 2:14)
69. the _____of Lebanon (Isa. 14:8)
70. so will I multiply the seed of _____, my servant (Jer. 33:22)
71. for my yoke is _____(Matt. 11:30)
73. the Lord said unto _____(Job 1:7)
76. who is worthy to _____the book (Rev. 5:2)

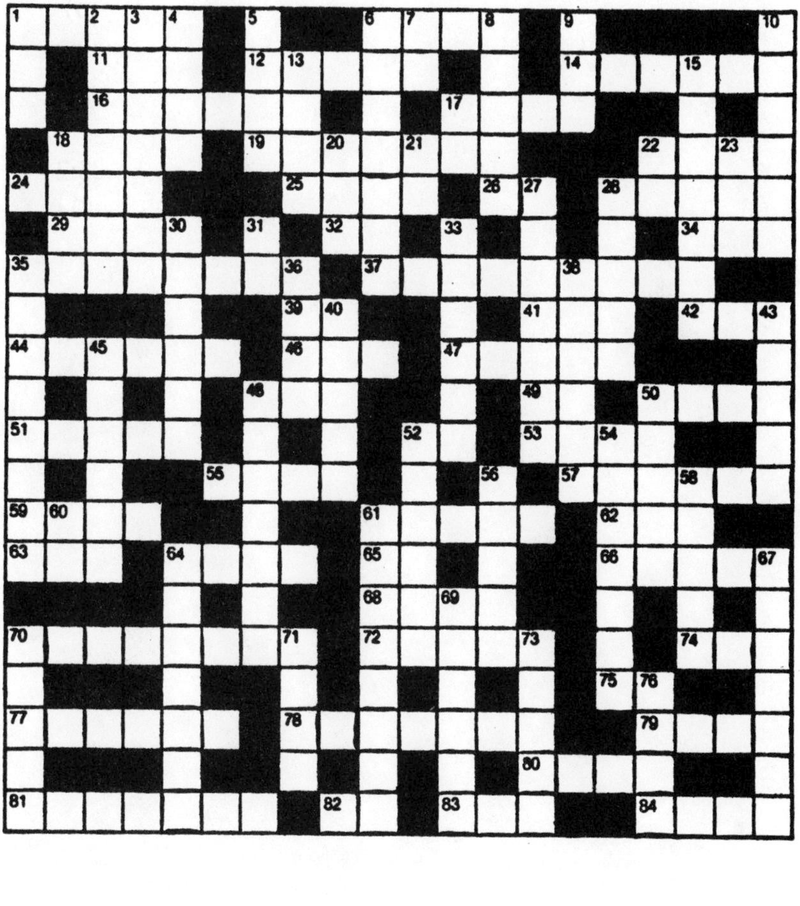

ANSWERS

CHAPTER 1

NUMBERS, DATES, AND OTHER
IMPORTANT FACTS

1.   *c* (39 in the Old Testament, 27 in the New Testament)
2.   *c* (Exod. 12:41)
3.   *d* (Gen. 5:20)
4.   *d* (Gen. 5:4)
5.   *c* (Gen. 7:24)
6.   *b* (Judg. 7:1–8)
7.   *c* (Isa. 38:5)
8.   *b* (Gen. 1:1, John 1:1)
9.   *b* (176 verses)
10. *d* (2 verses)
11. *c*
12. *a* (John 11:35)
13. *b* (Matt. 7:12)
14. *d*
15. *d* (Judg. 9:15)
16. *a*
17. *b* (I Kings 9:16)
18. *a* (Gen. 44:17)
19. *b* (Judg. 14:8)
20. *d* (Gen. 6:15)
21. *d* (Exod. 12:37)
22. *a*
23. *a,b,d* (Purim is mentioned in Esther 9:26)
24. *d*

THE BOOKS OF THE BIBLE

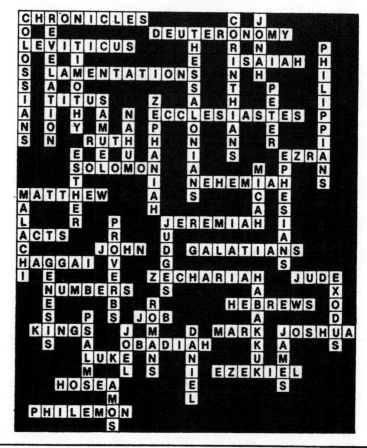

UNSCRAMBLING TWO BIBLICAL LISTS

a. Ⓣ R U M P Ⓔ T
b. P S A L T Ⓔ R Ⓨ
c. Ⓗ A R Ⓟ
d. Ⓣ Ⓘ M B Ⓡ E L
e. Ⓢ T R I N G E Ⓓ
   Ⓘ N S T Ⓡ U M Ⓔ N T S
f. Ⓞ R G Ⓐ N S
g. C Ⓨ M B A Ⓛ S

P R A I S E   Y E   T H E   L O R D

SPIRITUAL GIFTS

a. W I (S) D O (M)
b. K N O W L E D G (E)
c. (F) A I T H
d. H E A L (I) N G
e. M I R (A) C L E (S)
f. P (R) O (P) H E C Y
g. D I (S) C E R N M E N (T)
h. T O N (G) U E S
i. (I) N T E R P R E (T) A T (I) O N

There are diversities of: G I F T S but the S A M E
S P I R I T

25.	c (Gen. 7:1–3)
26.	b (Esther 9:26)
27.	d
28.	b
29.	b (Mark 6:3)
30.	b (nothing mentioned between age 12 at the temple and His baptism at age 30)
31.	c (Luke 2:41–52)
32.	c (John 19:23–24)
33.	d (Luke 10:1)
34.	c (Matt. 18:21,22)
35.	b (Matt. 26:15)
36.	b (a: Rev. 8:2; c: Rev. 5:1; d: Rev. 15:7)
37.	a
38.	a & d
39.	a (John 13:26)
40.	d (Matt. 18:3)
41.	a (Matt. 21:7–9)
42.	a (Acts 28:30,31; Paul wrote many of his epistles in Rome.)
43.	a (Luke 15:7)
44.	b (Luke 12:27)

CHAPTER 2
WHO'S WHO: THE FAMOUS AND THE FORGOTTEN

45. *d* (Exod. 3:4)
46. *b* (Job 3:3)
47. *b* (Exod. 2:22)
48. *a* (Exod. 6:20; his parents were Amram and Jochebed, a nephew-aunt relationship.)
49. *c* (Gen. 32:24–30)
50. *c* (I Kings 10:7)
51. *b* (Ruth 4:10)
52. *d* (Deut. 32:10)
53. *b* (Josh. 6:22)
54. *a* (Num. 27:22–23)
55. *d* (Gen. 19:26)
56. *d* (II Kings 11:3)
57. *b* (I Kings 4:30–32)
58. *d* (Exod. 2:7–9)
59. *d* (I Kings 22:41–45)
60. *a* (II Kings 24:10–11)

WHO'S WHO IN THE BOOK OF GENESIS (Part 1)

1. *k* (Gen. 17:17, 21:2)
2. *e* (Gen. 5:27)
3. *h* (Gen. 44)
4. *l* (Gen. 24:17, 51)
5. *j* (Gen. 9:20–27)
6. *c* (Gen. 25:34)
7. *b* (Gen. 22:9–14)
8. *d* (Gen. 6:13,18)
9. *f* (Gen. 12:4)
10. *i* (Gen. 16:11,21:14, 20)
11. *a* (Gen. 28:10–12)
12. *m* (Gen. 4:25)
13. *g* (Gen. 19:1)

WHO'S WHO IN THE BOOK OF GENESIS (Part 2)

1. *j* (Gen. 37:5–8)
2. *d* (Gen. 5:24)
3. *f* (Gen. 20:1–4)
4. *h* (Gen. 16:1–4,15)
5. *k* (Gen. 48:8–20)
6. *l* (Gen. 34:1–29)
7. *i* (Gen. 29:23–25)
8. *b* (Gen. 37:21–22)
9. *m* (Gen. 39:1–20)
10. *g* (Gen. 38:1–10)
11. *a* (Gen. 14:18)
12. *e* (Gen. 38:11–30)
13. *c* (Gen. 25:1)

THE EIGHTEEN KINGS WHO RULED THE NORTHERN KINGDOM OF ISRAEL

Ahab	(I Kings 16:29)	Jeroboam	(II Kings 14:23)
Ahaziah	(I Kings 22:51)	Menahem	(II Kings 15:17)
Baasha	(I Kings 15:33)	Nadab	(I Kings 15:25)
Elah	(I Kings 16:8)	Omri	(I Kings 16:23)
Hoshea	(II Kings 17:1)	Pekah	(II Kings 15:27)
Jehoahaz	(II Kings 13:1)	Shallum	(II Kings 15:13)
Jehoash	(II Kings 12:1)	Pekahiah	(II Kings 15:23)
Jehoram	(II Kings 3:1)	Zachariah	(II Kings 15:8)
Jehu	(II Kings 10:36)	Zimri	(I Kings 16:15)

61. *b* (Hos. 1:2–3)	69. *c* (Matt. 21:12–13)
62. *c* (Gen. 29:15–30)	70. *a* (Acts 13:36, 50)
63. *a* (Num. 14:6–8)	71. *b* (Luke 1:57–60)
64. *b* (Gen. 14:18; Heb.	72. *a* (Mark 14:3–8)
5:10)	
65. *a* (Dan. 5)	73. *b* (Luke 1:41)
66. *b* (I Sam. 10:17–27)	74. *a* (John 19:25)
67. *a* (Job 2:11)	75. *b* (John 3:3)
68. *d* (Neh. 2)	76. *d* (Matt. 8:5–10)

FAMOUS DATES

1. David and Michal (I Sam. 17:25, I Sam. 18:27)
2. Samson and Delilah (Judg. 16)
3. Rebekah and Isaac (Gen. 24:14, 51)
4. Ruth and Boaz (Ruth 3)
5. Ahab and Jezebel (I Kings 19:1–3)
6. Hosea and Gomer (Hos. 1:2)
7. Ananias and Sapphira (Acts 5:1–10)
8. Adam and Eve (Gen. 2:21–25)
9. Ahasuerus and Esther (Esther 2)
10. Jacob and Leah (Gen. 29:25)

BIG THREES

1. True. He often asked the three of them to come when he left the other desciples behind. (Matt. 26:37)
2. True. And who are we to say it wasn't an improvement? (Dan. 1:7)
3. False. They were sons of Benjamin. (Gen. 46:21)
4. False. David had Uriah killed so Bathsheba could be his, and Uriah didn't have time to argue over much of anything. (II Sam. 11)
5. True. As Noah's sons, they got a ride; however, they did learn a lot about cleaning up after animals. (Gen. 7:13)

6. False. With their famous wives, these three partiarchs begat the nation of Israel. (Abraham: Gen. 11:29, 16:3, 25:1; Isaac: Gen. 24:67; Jacob: Gen. 29:25, 28, 30:4,9)
7. True. If they had patents, they'd be rich. Jubal invented musical instruments (Gen. 4:20–22); Jabal, tents; Tubal Cain, crafts.
8. False. Jacob's father-in-law falsified his work contract, and Jacob expected his brother to try to murder him at their reunion. (Gen. 27–31)
9. True. He stayed with them in Bethany when he was in Jerusalem, and he raised Lazarus from the dead. (John 11:5)

77.	a (Matt. 3:7)	83.	a (Matt. 27:15–22)
78.	c (Luke 24:13–31)	84.	c (Acts 8:1)
79.	d (Acts 9:3–6)	85.	b (Matt. 9:9–11)
80.	c (Acts 4:1–18)	86.	a (Luke 10:25–37)
81.	d (Luke 23:50)	87.	c (Mark 3:16–17)
82.	a (Matt. 2:1–12)	88.	d (Acts 1:23–26)

WHO'S WHO IN THE BOOK OF ACTS (Part 1)

1.	f (Acts 9:10–19)	8.	e (Acts 5:33–42)
2.	g (Acts 7)	9.	b (Acts 16:19–25)
3.	h (Acts 8:26–40)	10.	l (Acts 16:14–15)
4.	c (Acts 13:1–3; 15:36–41)	11.	m (Acts 26)
5.	k (Acts 10)	12.	i (Acts 4:5–12)
6.	a (Acts 8:9–13)	13.	d (Acts 9:36–42)
7.	j (Acts 18:1–4)		

WHO'S WHO IN THE BOOK OF ACTS (Part 2)

1. *f* (Acts 24:27)
2. *d* (Acts 17:33)
3. *i* (Acts 1:26)
4. *j* (Acts 20:9)
5. *h* (Acts 12:12–17)
6. *m* (Acts 5:7–11)
7. *k* (Acts 17:5–9)
8. *l* (Acts 19:13–16)
9. *g* (Acts 18:24–28)
10. *e* (Acts 18:17)
11. *c* (Acts 13:8–11)
12. *a* (Acts 28:7–8)
13. *b* (Acts 21:10–14)

SHEPHERD, SCRIBE, & OTHER BIBLICAL OCCUPATIONS

1. *k* (Acts 10:1)
2. *h* (Ezra 7:12)
3. *o* (I Sam. 16:11–13)
4. *c* (Acts 18:1–3)
5. *i* (II Sam. 11:15)
6. *s* (Amos 7:14)
7. *p* (Luke 16:20)
8. *j* (Luke 5:27)
9. *g* (Judg. 4:4)
10. *a* (Acts 21:10)
11. *r* (Josh. 2:1)
12. *q* (II Chron. 29:1)
13. *f* (Rev. 12:7)
14. *e* (Gen. 39:1)
15. *t* (Gen. 25:27)
16. *m* (Neh. 1:11)
17. *l* (Exod. 1:15)
18. *b* (Matt. 4:18)
19. *n* (II Kings 18:18)
20. *d* (Matt. 13:55)

PEOPLE IN THE BIBLE WHO WEPT

1. *n* (Acts 20:37)
2. *c* (John 20:11)
3. *g* (Gen. 21:16)
4. *f* (Lam. 2:11)
5. *i* (Rev. 5:4)
6. *p* (Luke 7:37–38)
7. *a* (Gen. 23:2)
8. *e* (I Sam. 20:41)
9. *o* (Esther 8:3)
10. *j* (Luke 23:28)
11. *h* (Acts 20:18,19)
12. *m* (Matt. 26:75)
13. *k* (Gen. 29:11)
14. *l* (Isa. 22:4)
15. *b* (Job 16:20)
16. *d* (Ezra 10:1)

CHAPTER 3
DECISIONS THAT SHAPED HISTORY

89. *b* (Judg. 21:25)
90. *a* (Josh. 7:1, 4, 5, 20, 21)
91. *c* (Judg. 6:36–40)
92. *a* (I Sam. 9:3–21)
93. *b* (Gen. 37:3–4)
94. *a* (Exod. 32:19, 20)
95. *b* (Dan. 1:8–16)
96. *d* (Dan. 6:24)
97. *c* (Num. 13:16)
98. *b* (Esther 3:5–6)
99. *d* (Gen. 29:5–28)
100. *b* (Esther 2:10)
101. *a* (II Sam. 6:2–12)
102. *d* (II Chron. 36:22–23)
103. *b* (Gen. 25:27–28)
104. *a* (I Kings 3:16–28)
105. *d* (Gen. 6:14)

DECISIONS, DECISIONS

1. *p* (Gen. 19:26)
2. *s* (Matt. 26:14–16)
3. *f* (Exod. 32:1–4)
4. *j* (Jon. 1:1–3)
5. *a* (Luke 10:38–40)
6. *d* (Esther 7)
7. *q* (Exod. 2:5–10)
8. *k* (I Sam. 28:7–10)
9. *l* (II Kings 11:1–3)
10. *i* (Hos. 1:2–3, 3:1–3)
11. *r* (Dan. 1:8)
12. *c* (Matt. 9:9)
13. *m* (Matt. 14:3–12)
14. *e* (Josh. 7:18–21)
15. *g* (Ruth 1:16–19)
16. *h* (John 12:3)
17. *o* (Acts 16:25–29)

18.   *t* (II Kings 6:18–23)
19.   *b* (Gen. 45:9)
20.   *n* (Luke 8:1–3)

EXIT, STAGE RIGHT

1. *c, vi*   (Acts 9:19–25)
2. *e, ix*   (Jon. 1:13–17)
3. *g, x*   (Gen. 19:15–24)
4. *k, ii*   (Gen. 3:22–24)
5. *i, xii*   (Acts 1:6–12)
6. *l, iii*   (II Kings 2:6–11)
7. *d, viii*   (Judg. 16:21–31)
8. *a, v*   (Acts 7:54–60)
9. *j, vii*   (Exod. 14:21–22)
10. *f, xi*   (Gen. 37:25–28)
11. *h, i*   (Josh. 2:15–18)
12. *b, iv*   (Mark 14:32, 52)

---

106.   *d* (Matt. 1:20)
107.   *a* (Mark 3:21–22)
108.   *c* (Luke 2:1–5)
109.   *b* (Acts 8:26–39)
110.   *b* (John 11:31–35)
111.   *c* (Mark 10:17–22)
112.   *d* (Matt. 27:26)
113.   *d* (Mark 2:17)
114.   *c* (Matt. 2:16)
115.   *d* (Matt. 26:48–49)
116.   *c* (Matt. 27:5)
117.   *c* (John 13:5–15)
118.   *a* (Matt. 27:5–7)
119.   *b* (Luke 23:1–2)
120.   *d* (Matt. 27:24–25)
121.   *c* (Acts 27:29–44)

A HARMONY OF THE GOSPELS

	MATT.	MARK	LUKE	JOHN
1.			2:8–20	
2.	2:1–12			
3.	3:13–17	1:9–11	3:21–22	
4.	4:1–11	1:12–13	4:1–13	
5.	6:9–13		11:2–4	
6.				3:1–21
7.				4:7–38
8.	14:13–21	6:30–44	9:10–17	6:1–14
9.	14:22–32	6:45–52		6:15–21
10.	17:1–13	9:2–13	9:28:36	
11.			10:25–37	
12.	19:16–30	10:17–31	18:18–30	
13.				11:17–44
14.	22:35–40	12:28–34		
15.			19:1–10	
16.	21:1–11	11:1–11	19:29–44	12:12–19
17.	25:1–13			
18.	26:26–29	14:22–25	22:15–20	
19.	27:35–44	15:24–32	23:33–38	19:18–27
20.		16:12–13	24:13–35	

CHAPTER 4
MEMORABLE COMMENTS

1.	*h* (Philippians 4:13)	9.	*f* (Romans 6:23)
2.	*j* (Ecclesiastes 3:1)	10.	*b* (Hebrews 11:1)
3.	*l* (Matthew 6:33)	11.	*g* (John 15:13)
4.	*a* (Jeremiah 33:3)	12.	*n* (Revelation 3:20)
5.	*k* (James 1:19)	13.	*o* (Psalm 19:1)
6.	*c* (Genesis 3:19)	14.	*i* (Acts 16:31
7.	*m* (I John 1:9)	15.	*d* (Ezekiel 37:4)
8.	*e* (Proverbs 3:5)		

122.	*b* (Gen. 4:9)	128.	*c* (Ruth 1:11–16)
123.	*c* (I Sam. 17:44)	129.	*d* (Gen. 2:18–21)
124.	*c* (Num. 22:28)	130.	*d* (II Sam. 18:33)
125.	*a* (Exod. 3:5)	131.	*b* (Prov. 25:25)
126.	*a* (Exod. 20:5)	132.	*b* (Prov. 18:7)
127.	*a* (Dan. 5:25–28)	133.	*c* (Jer. 15:16)

I WISH I'D SAID THAT!

1. Adam to Eve on their mutual discovery of each other. (Gen. 2:23)
2. God to Moses, after Moses asked what name he should use to refer to God. (Exod. 3:14)
3. Aaron to the Israelites when he blessed them; the instructions to do so came directly from God. (Num. 6:24–26)
4. Delilah to Samson every time he fell asleep and she tried a new way to curb his enormous strength. (Judg. 16:9, 12, 14, 20)
5. Ruth to Naomi when she decided to go with her mother-in-law after her husband's death. (Ruth 1:16)
6. David to Jonathan in the song David wrote after Jonathan was killed. (II Sam. 1:26)

7. Solomon to the two women who came to him, both claiming to be the mother of the same child. (I Kings 3:25)
8. Job to the messenger who came telling of his children's sudden deaths. (Job 1:21)
9. Herodias' daughter to her uncle Herod after she danced at his party and was promised whatever she asked for. (Matt. 14:8)
10. Jesus to Peter, when Peter told him not to speak of his impending death. (Matt. 16:23)

THE LORD'S PRAYER

THE LAST SEVEN SAYINGS OF JESUS ON THE CROSS

1. forgive them/not what they do (Luke 23:34)
2. To day/in paradise (Luke 23:43)
3. behold thy son/behold thy mother (John 19:26,27)
4. thou forsaken me (Mark 15:34)
5. thirst (John 19:28)
6. is finished (John 19:30)
7. into thy hands/spirit (Luke 23:46)

134.	*b* (Luke 4:4)		146.	*a* (Matt. 6:24)
135.	*c* (John 14:2)		147.	*a* (Luke 7:48–49)
136.	*d* (John 1:45–49)		148.	*c* (Matt. 9:6–7)
137.	*a* (Luke 23:42)		149.	*c* (Matt. 6:28)
138.	*c* (John 2:4)		150.	*b* (Psalm 22:1)
139.	*d* (Mark 10:25)		151.	*d* (Acts 3:6)
140.	*a* (I John 3:15)		152.	*a* (John 15:5)
141.	*c* (Mark 12:43–44)		153.	*b* (Rev. 22:20)
142.	*d* (Luke 23)		154.	*d* (Mark 4:10–12)
143.	*d* (Luke 18:9–14)		155.	*c* (Luke 4:9–12)
144.	*b* (Matt. 3:17)		156.	*b* (Luke 2:34–35)
145.	*a* (Matt. 22:15–21)		157.	*d* (Matt. 5:28)

THE QUOTABLE JESUS

1.	*e* (Matt. 4:3–5)
2.	*f* (Matt. 21:19)
3.	*g* (Luke 2:48–49)
4.	*j* (John 20:16–18)
5.	*b* (John 13:26–27)
6.	*d* (John 18:35–36)
7.	*a* (Matt. 16:23)
8.	*h* (John 14:5–6)
9.	*m* (Mark 10:17–22)
10.	*q* (Luke 23:39–43)
11.	*o* (Luke 19:10)
12.	*p* (Luke 24:18–27)
13.	*r* (Matt. 22:34–39)
14.	*l* (John 3:1–3)
15.	*n* (John 14:8–9)
16.	*i* (John 11:24–26)
17.	*s* (Matt. 11:2–6)
18.	*c* (John 8:3–11)
19.	*t* (Mark 10:46–52)
20.	*k* (John 4:9–24)

CHAPTER 5
PROPHECIES AND PROMISES

UNSCRAMBLING ISAIAH'S PROPHECY

a. R E (J) E C T E D
b. (S) O R R O W S
c. G R (I) E F
d. D E S P I (S) E D
e. T (R) A N S G R E (S) S I O N S
f. I N I Q (U) I (T) I E S
g. P E A (C) E
h. S T R I P (E) S
i. (H) E A L E D

J E S U S   C H R I S T

FIND THE 20 MISSING PROPHETS

BLESSED ARE...
(Matt. 5:3-12)

1. *d/i*
2. *g*
3. *h*
4. *a*
5. *c*

6. *b*
7. *f*
8. *i/d*
9. *e*

---

158. *b* (Gen. 15:5)
159. *a* (Gen. 9:11-13)
160. *b* (I Kings 3:11-14)
161. *c* (Exod. 6:4)
162. *b* (Rev. 16:16-17)
163. *c* (Luke 17:24-37)
164. *c* (Matt. 26:26-28)
165. *b* (Matt. 7:24-25)

END TIMES PROPHECIES

1. days perilous (II Tim. 3:1)
2. kingdom against kingdom (Matt. 24:7)
3. rumors/of wars (Matt. 24:6)
4. day/thief/night (I Thess. 5:2)
5. sin/be/revealed (II Thess. 2:3)
6. day/hour/Father (Matt. 24:36)
7. heaven/shout (I Thess. 4:16)
8. lightning/coming/Son (Matt. 24:27)
9. sound/trumpet (Matt. 24:31)
10. dead/rise first (I Thess. 4:16)
11. caught/meet/Lord (I Thess. 4:17)
12. sun be darkened (Matt. 24:29)
13. heavens/earth/righteousness (II Pet. 3:13)
14. lake/fire/ brimstone (Rev. 20:10)
15. tears/eyes/death/sorrow/crying/pain/passed away (Rev. 21:4)

ISAIAH: A DOUBLE ACROSTIC

A. shield

B. father
C. Abraham/Ishmael
D. Slay my

E. tooth
F. To many
G. other
H. in law
I. midday
J. tossings
K. Canst thou
L. washest
M. go mourning
N. didst divide

O. youth
P. joy
Q. wroth
R. doeth the will
S. that labour and are heavy laden
T. build
U. oath
V. waste
W. vine
X. condemnation
Y. sufferings
Z. tattlers
AA. prisoner
BB. holy
CC. magog

The verse in the grid is found in Isaiah 12:1-2:

And in that day thou shalt say, O Lord, I will praise thee: though thou wast angry with me, thine anger is turned away, and thou comfortedst me. Behold, God is my salvation; I will trust, and not be afraid: for the Lord Jehovah is my strength and my song; he also is become my salvation.

CHAPTER 6
COMMANDMENTS AND CURSES

166. *a* (Gen. 22:1–2)
167. *d* (Num. 21:6–9)
168. *a* (Gen. 17:9–11)
169. *b* (Num. 12)
170. *c* (II Kings 2:23–24)
171. *b* (Exod. 21:32)
172. *a* (Exod. 32:27–28)
173. *b* (Gen. 3:16)
174. *c* (Gen. 18:32,9,19:14)
175. *a* (Deut. 22:28–29)
176. *c* (Deut. 24:5)
177. *a* (Jon. 3)
178. *d* (The Talmud had its origin in the oral teaching of rabbis over many centuries. It is an open-ended dialogue given to the continuous examination of the Torah, or the first five books of the Old Testament.)

NEW TESTAMENT COMMANDMENTS

1 a. heart
  b. soul
  c. mind
  d. neighbor
  e. thyself

(Matt. 22:37–39)

2 a. truth
  b. righteousness
  c. gospel of peace
  d. faith
  e. salvation
  f. spirit

(Eph. 6:14–17)

3 a. word
  b. conversation
  c. charity
  d. spirit
  e. faith
  f. purity

(I Tim. 4:12)

4 a. true
  b. honest
  c. just
  d. pure
  e. lovely
  f. good report
  g. virtue
  h. praise

(Phil. 4:8)

186

THE TEN COMMANDMENTS
(Exod. 20:3-17)

1. Thou shalt have no other gods before me.
2. Thou shalt not make unto thee any graven image.
3. Thou shalt not take the name of the Lord thy God in vain.
4. Remember the sabbath day, to keep it holy.
5. Honour thy father and thy mother.
6. Thou shalt not kill.
7. Thou shalt not commit adultery.
8. Thou shalt not steal.
9. Thou shalt not bear false witness.
10. Thou shalt not covet.

THE WORKS OF THE FLESH AND THE FRUIT OF THE SPIRIT

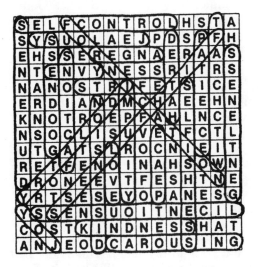

179. c (Mark 10:9)
180. a (Luke 3:19)
181. d (Matt. 22:35–40)
182. c (Mark 3:1–6)
183. c (Matt. 6:1–4)
184. d (Luke 9:3)

A COMMANDMENT: A DOUBLE ACROSTIC

A. fruit
B. strange
C. hang
D. loveth
E. thy loins
F. return thither
G. they than gold
H. in battle
I. will lift up mine eyes unto the
J. whole land
K. vomit
L. that wait
M. commandeth

N. didst commit
O. shall stand
P. dash
Q. Hallowed
R. who hath ears
S. hand/God
T. hath holpen
U. cast
V. honesty

W. to day
X. lusts
Y. keys/hell
Z. month

The quote in the grid is found in Matthew 22:37–40:

Thou shalt love the Lord thy God with all thy heart, and with all thy soul, and with all thy mind. This is the first and great commandment. And the second is like unto it, Thou shalt love thy neighbour as thyself. On these two commandments hang all the law and the prophets.

CHAPTER 7
SINS AND OTHER FAULTS

185.   *a* (Judg. 16:5)
186.   *d* (Gen. 19:32)
187.   *a* (Gen. 11:4–6)
188.   *c* (I Kings 1:1–4)
189.   *b* (Gen. 3:12, 17)
190.   *d* (Gen. 39)
191.   *d* (Exod. 2:11–12)
192. *a,b,c* (Judg. 16:6–19)
193.   *b* (with Hagar) (Gen. 16)
194.   *a* (Jon. 2)
195.   *c* (I Sam. 4:3, 10)
196.   *c* (II Kings 9:30–33)
197.   *d* (I Kings 16:30–31)
198.   *b* (I Sam. 8:1–5)
199.   *b* (Gen. 4:4–8)
200.   *c* (I Kings 11:4)

SINNERS ANONYMOUS

1.   *f*, xi   (Gen. 3:14, 15)
2.   *h*, vii   (Acts 5:10)
3.   *d*, xii   (II Sam. 12:7–12)
4.   *k*, ii   (Exod. 7–12)
5.   *p*, xiii   (Num. 14)
6.   *l*, i   (Gen. 18,19)
7.   *b*, ix   (II Sam. 6:16–23)
8.   *o*, vi   (Luke 1:11–20)
9.   *c*, v   (I Sam. 2–41)
10. *n*, viii   (II Sam. 13)
11. *e*, xv   (Luke 10:40–42)
12. *m*, xvi   (Num. 22:31–34)
13. *a*, iii   (Jon. 1)
14. *i*, iv   (I Sam. 13:9–14)
15. *j*, xiv   (Num. 12)
16. *g*, x   (II Kings 9:30–37)

---

201. *c* (II Sam. 12–18)
202. *a* (I Sam. 2:12–17)
203. *c* (a: Gen. 34:25–27;
    b: Gen. 38;
    d: Gen. 37)
204. *d* (a: Gen. 27;
    b: Gen. 27:41;
    c: Gen. 26:34)
205. *d* (II Sam. 11)
206. *a* (I Sam. 15)
207. *c* (Gen. 27:15–16)
208. *b* (II Sam. 24:1–17)
209. *a* (Gen. 9:21)
210. *c* (Jonah 1:1–3)
211. *c* (I Kings 21:6–13)
212. *b* (Matt. 18:6)

I HAVE BUT ONE REGRET...

1. Adam and Eve (Gen. 3)
2. Jonah (Jon. 1)
3. Lot's wife (Gen. 19:26)
4. Noah's neighbors (Gen. 6 and 7)
5. Uzzah (II Sam. 6:6–7; also assorted heathen thieves)
6. Pilate (Matt. 27)
7. John Mark (Acts 15:37–40)
8. Jezebel (I Kings 21)
9. Goliath (I Sam. 17:42–43)
10. Absolom (II Sam. 18:9–15)
11. Bathsheba (II Sam. 11)
12. King Saul (I Sam. 13:8–14)
13. Samson (Judg. 16:19)
14. Simon Peter (Matt. 14:25–32)
15. Haman (Esther 7)
16. Herod (Matt. 14)
17. Jacob (Gen. 37)
18. Achan (Josh. 7)

213. *b* (Luke 22:45–46)
214. *b* (John 20:24–29)
215. *d* (Mark 6:22–28)
216. *b* (Matt. 14:29–31)
217. *a* (Luke 22:3–4)
218. *c* (Mark 14:51–52)
219. *b* (Matt. 26:56)
220. *a* (John 18:10–11)
221. *b* (Matt. 26:69–74)
222. *c* (Matt. 20:20–21)
223. *d* (Acts 15:36–41)
224. *c* (Rev. 3:14–16)

THE WEAKNESS OF THE FLESH: A DOUBLE ACROSTIC

A. third day
B. art thou
C. flaming sword
D. thigh
E. witch
F. serve the Lord
G. shave
H. hottest
I. Bath
J. side
K. mindful
L. the fool hath
M. that took me out
N. shall direct
O. balm

P. swords
Q. the evil thereof
R. doth come
S. foot offend
T. daily
U. his hire
V. own mouth
W. Jew/Gentile
X. though
Y. whit
Z. bond
AA. wine
BB. I wish
CC. would thou

The quote in the grid is found in Romans 7:19, 24–25:

For the good that I would I do not: but the evil which I would not, that I do . . . O wretched man that I am! who shall deliver me from the body of this death? I thank God through Jesus Christ our Lord. So then with the mind I myself serve the law of God; but with the flesh the law of sin.

CHAPTER 8
PLACES THAT TIME PASSED BY

225.	*b* (Gen 8:4)		229.	*a* (Gen. 32:22–32)
226.	*d* (Ps. 2:6)		230.	*c* (I Kings 10:1–13)
227.	*b* (Isa. 3:8–24)		231.	*b* (I Sam. 17:4)
228.	*b* (Judg. 4:5)		232.	*c* (Ruth 1:1–7)

SUCH MEMORABLE PLACES

1. Bethel
2. Bethlehem
3. Jerusalem
4. Gog
5. Magog
6. Sodom
7. Nile
8. Canaan
9. Ur
10. Babylon
11. Jericho
12. Sinai
13. Ararat
14. Eden
15. Golgotha
16. Paradise
17. Hell
18. Tarsus
19. Nazareth
20. Galilee
21. Damascus
22. Athens
23. Patmos
24. Egypt
25. Tyre
26. Antioch

---

233. *d* (Matt. 11:20–24)
234. *a*
235. *c* (Matt. 3:6)
236. *b* (Matt. 27:33–35)
237. *d* (Luke 19:1–4)
238. *a* (Acts 13:1–3)
239. *a* (Luke 24:13–35)
240. *b* (Acts 16:6–10)

CHAPTER 9
MIRACLES AND THE
SUPERNATURAL

241. *d* (Dan. 3:12–27)
242. *b* (Gen. 17:17, 18:12)
243. *a* (Gen. 40, 41:25)
244. *d* (Judg. 16:22–30)
245. *b* (I Kings 17:3–15)
246. *b* (Exod. 15:4–5)
247. *a* (Exod. 12:27)
248. *c* (Exod. 14:24)
249. *a* (II Kings 2:11)
250. *c* (a and b: I Sam. 5:2–9;
       d: I Sam. 6:19)
251. *b* (Exod. 7–12)
252. *d* (a: I Kings 18:20–44;
       b: II Kings 2:8;
       c: I Kings 17:14–16)

WHAT TO SAY TO A BURNING BUSH

1. *c*, iv   (Gen. 28:12–18)
2. *f*, x   (Exod. 3:4–5)
3. *g*, viii   (Isa. 6:1–7)
4. *j*, v   (Ezek. 1:26–3:3)
5. *h*, ix   (Acts 7:55–58)
6. *a*, ii   (Gen. 18:1–8)
7. *i*, i   (Gen. 3:8)
8. *d*, vii   (I Kings 19:9–14)
9. *b*, iii   (John 20:14–18)
10. *e*, vi   (Dan. 3:24–30)

1.	*e* (II Cor. 12:2)	10.	*g* (Acts 10:1–6)
2.	*l* (Dan. 2:31–35)	11.	*a* (Ezek. 37:1–10)
3.	*p* (Gen. 41:1–4)	12.	*n* (Luke 1:11–22)
4.	*q* (I Sam. 3:11–14)	13.	*d* (Gen. 17:19)
5.	*o* (Matt. 2:12)	14.	*f* (Rev. 4:1–6)
6.	*b* (Gen. 28:12)	15.	*m* (Acts 7:55)
7.	*c* (Acts 9:10–16)	16.	*j* (Dan. 9:20–27)
8.	*k* (I Kings 3:5)	17.	*i* (Acts 10:9–16)
9.	*r* (Gen. 37:5–11)	18.	*h* (Isa. 6:1)

253. *b* (Matt. 4:11)
254. *d* (Judg. 13:18)
255. *b* (a: Ezek. 17:3, c: Dan. 10:6; d: Ezek. 10:9–10)
256. *d* (a: Gen. 3;
      b: Matt. 4;
      c: John 13:27)
257. *d* (Acts 5:19; 12:7–11; the other three can be found in II Kings)
258. *a* (Mark 9:2–9)
259. *c* (Matt. 14:15–20; Mark 6:38–42; Luke 9:13–17; John 6:9–13)
260. *d* (Matt. 3:16–17)
261. *c* (Mark 5:17)
262. *b* (John 6:9–11)
263. *a* (Mark 8:23)
264. *a* (Luke 8:56)
265. *b* (Matt. 27:45)
266. *a* (Matt. 14:2)
267. *b* (Acts 16:19–34)
268. *d* (Mark 16:19)
269. *d* (Acts 2:3–4)
270. *c* (Acts 2:16–17; see also Joel 2:28–32)
271. *d* (John 6:13)
272. *a* (John 4:16–20)

CHAPTER 10
COMPLETE YOUR FAVORITE BIBLE PASSAGE

PSALM 23

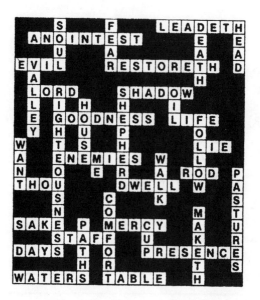

The <u>Lord</u> is my <u>shepherd</u>; I shall not <u>want</u>. He <u>maketh</u> me to <u>lie</u> down in green <u>pastures</u>: he <u>leadeth</u> me beside the still <u>waters</u>. He <u>restoreth</u> my <u>soul</u>: he leadeth <u>me</u> in the <u>paths</u> of <u>righteousness</u> for his name's <u>sake</u>. Yea, though I <u>walk</u> through the <u>valley</u> of the <u>shadow</u> of <u>death</u>, I will <u>fear</u> no <u>evil</u>: for <u>thou</u> art with me; thy <u>rod</u> and thy <u>staff</u> they <u>comfort</u> me. Thou preparest a <u>table</u> before me in the <u>presence</u> of mine <u>enemies</u>: thou <u>anointest</u> my <u>head</u> with <u>oil</u>; my <u>cup</u> runneth over. Surely <u>goodness</u> and <u>mercy</u> shall <u>follow</u> me all the <u>days</u> of my <u>life</u>: and I will <u>dwell</u> in the <u>house</u> of the Lord for ever.

1.	*g* (Prov. 15:1)
2.	*k* (Prov. 25:11)
3.	*j* (Prov. 15:13)
4.	*h* (Prov. 22:1)
5.	*o* (Prov. 1:7)
6.	*n* (Prov. 29:18)
7.	*m* (Prov. 27:5)
8.	*a* (Prov. 25:14)
9.	*b* (Prov. 29:11)
10.	*d* (Prov. 28:26)
11.	*i* (Prov. 31:30)
12.	*f* (Prov. 4:18)
13.	*e* (Prov. 11:30)
14.	*l* (Prov. 12:4)
15.	*c* (Prov. 13:12)

IN PRAISE OF LOVE (CHARITY)

a. T O N G (U) E (S)
b. (A) N G E L S
c. C H A R (I) T Y
d. B (R) A S S
e. T I N K L (I) N G
f. (P) R O P H E C Y
g. M Y S (T) E R I E (S)
h. K N O W (L) E D (G) E
i. (F) A I T H
j. M O U N T A (I) N S
k. N O (T) H I N G

S P I R I T U A L   G I F T S

273.	*a* (Prov. 19:4)
274.	*a,b,c* (Prov. 15:13; 15:15; 17:22)
275.	*b* (Ps. 127:4–5)
276.	*c* (Sol. 7:9)
277.	˒*d* (Prov. 7:22; see also verses 6–21)
278.	*b* (Heb. 11:1)
279.	*a* (II Cor. 9:7)
280.	*b* (Sol. 2:12)
281.	*b* (Matt. 6:33)
282.	*d* (John 15:13)

283.   c (John 1:14)
284.   a (I Cor. 15:55)

TEST YOUR KNOWLEDGE OF PAULINE THEOLOGY

1. *e* For the <u>wages</u> of sin is <u>death</u>; but the <u>gift</u> of God is <u>eternal</u> <u>life</u>.
2. *c* Therefore being justified by <u>faith</u>, we have <u>peace</u> with God.
3. *i* All things <u>work</u> together for <u>good</u> to them that <u>love</u> God.
4. *k* Whosoever shall <u>call</u> upon the <u>name</u> of the Lord shall be <u>saved</u>.
5. *f* For the <u>good</u> that I would I <u>do</u> <u>not</u>.
6. *b* There is no <u>respect</u> of persons with <u>God</u>.
7. *o* Make not <u>provision</u> for the <u>flesh</u>, to fulfil the <u>lusts</u> thereof.
8. *n* Let every <u>soul</u> be <u>subject</u> unto the higher <u>powers</u>.
9. *a* The <u>just</u> shall live by <u>faith</u>.
10. *h* For we are saved by <u>hope</u>.
11. *m* So we, being <u>many</u>, are one <u>body</u> in Christ.
12. *l* Present your <u>bodies</u> a living <u>sacrifice</u>, holy, <u>acceptable</u> unto <u>God</u>.
13. *g* There is therefore now no <u>condemnation</u> to them which are in <u>Christ</u> <u>Jesus</u>.
14. *d* We are <u>buried</u> with him by <u>baptism</u> into death.
15. *j* I am persuaded, that neither <u>death</u>, nor <u>life</u>, nor <u>angels</u>, nor <u>principalities</u>, nor <u>powers</u>, nor <u>things</u> present, nor <u>things</u> to come, nor <u>height</u>, nor <u>depth</u>, nor any other <u>creature</u>, shall be able to <u>separate</u> us from the <u>love</u> of God.

A SCRIPTURE-VERSE
CROSSWORD PUZZLE

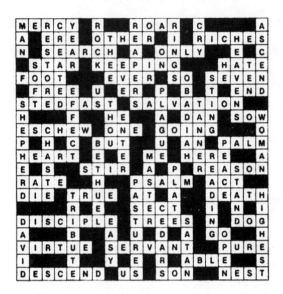

Answers to Photographs

1. Page 1: Because the brothers envied Joseph.

2. Page 17: Adam registers man's first complaint to God.

3. Page 39: The married woman was Bathsheba.

4. Page 55: Noah brings the animals on board the Ark.

5. Page 75: Just another swordfight in the Bible.

6. Page 89: Delila wants to cut Samson's hair to weaken him.

7. Page 105: A chariot sideshow in the movie Ten Commandments.

8. Page 127: The wicked people of Sodom.

9. Page 137: The Roman soldiers.

10. Page 151: Young David preparing to throw a stone at Goliath.